TRACING
PERSONAL EXPANSION

Reading Selected Novels as
Modern African *Bildungsromane*

Walter P. Collins, III

University Press of America,® Inc.
Lanham · Boulder · New York · Toronto · Oxford

Copyright © 2006 by
University Press of America,® Inc.
4501 Forbes Boulevard
Suite 200
Lanham, Maryland 20706
UPA Acquisitions Department (301) 459-3366

PO Box 317
Oxford
OX2 9RU, UK

Library of Congress Control Number: 2006923746
ISBN-13: 978-0-7618-3483-0 (paperback : alk. paper)
ISBN-10: 0-7618-3483-4 (paperback : alk. paper)

⊖™ The paper used in this publication meets the minimum
requirements of American National Standard for Information
Sciences—Permanence of Paper for Printed Library Materials,
ANSI Z39.48—1984

For Ashley and Jack

Contents

Foreword

African women's writing in European languages emerged on the international literary scene in the 1970's and 1980's. Prior to this period, African and Western critics alike were principally focused on writing by male authors. As Walt Collins points out here, *Efuru* by Nigerian Flora Nwapa and *The Promised Land* by Kenyan Grace Ogot were published in 1966, but these works were eclipsed by the critical attention paid to writing by their respective countrymen Chinua Achebe and Ngugi wa Thiong'o. As Florence Stratton demonstrates in her book *Contemporary African Literature and the Politics of Gender*, this trend was endemic to the field of African literary studies well into the 1990's, a period which finally saw the publication of a number of important studies on African women's writing by such scholars as d'Almeida, Boyce-Davies, Cazenave, and Stratton herself.

Concurrent with the emergence of African women writers was the development of Women's Studies in Europe and particularly of Women's Studies programs on the campuses of universities in North America and Europe. Also coincident with this emergence of African women's writing in European languages (and consequently in the consciousnesses of Western scholars and critics not proficient in African-language oral and written literatures) was the rising interest in women's autobiography and the novel of development, or *Bildungsroman*, as feminist critics across the board began to explore the inscription of female subjectivity, agency, and identity in autobiographical and semi-autobiographical works by women. At the same time, black feminist theorists and critics began to call attention to the inadequacies of mainstream feminist theory and criticism for understanding discrimination faced by women of color based on the categories of gender, class, and particularly race.

As Walt Collins shows in his introductory chapter on the *Bildungsroman*, Western feminist critics who began to reexamine this genre demonstrated that the "novel of development" could also foreground female protagonists and feminist issues. The groundbreaking collection entitled *The Voyage In: Fictions of Female Development*, edited by Elizabeth Abel, Marianne Hirsch, and Elizabeth Langland and published in 1983, contained sixteen essays about the female *bildungsroman*. One of them, Mary Helen Washington 's "Plain, Black, and Decently Wild" was about Pulitzer prize-winning poet Gwendolyn Brooks' *Maud Martha* (1953).Washington demonstrates in her essay that while Ralph Ellison's contemporaneous *Invisble Man* received considerable acclaim, Brooks' book was trivialized. While Ellison was heralded as a voice for his people in the

New Republic, The Nation, and *The New Yorker,* "no one in 1953 had more than six hundred words to say about the novel"(271).

A similar silencing is evident in literary portrayals of African women prior to their "coming to writing" in European languages in the 1960s. While Senegalese Annette Mbaye d'Erneville's first French-language collection of poetry, *Poèmes africains,* was published in 1965, it was her countryman Léopold Sédar Senghor's earlier vision of African woman as a symbol of Negritude that predominated. In his 1945 poem "Black Woman," Senghor described the black woman's "deep contralto voice" as "the spiritual song of the Beloved" (in Bâ, 190). However, as a "mouth that makes my mouth sing," the Beloved's voice is muted by that of the male poet. At the end of the poem, the "naked woman, black woman" crumbles "to dust to nourish the roots of life"(190).

It is the portrayal of "African Woman" as muted lover and mother and as the idealized symbol of African tradition and authenticity that Buchi Emecheta, Tsitsi Dangarembga, and Calixthe Beyala challenge in their writing. In this study of selected works by these writers as "novels of development," Walt Collins shows that these writers reveal a different reality. So doing, Collins contributes to an important critical conversation concerned with elaborating a more comprehensive definition of what constitutes contemporary "African literature," a literature composed by men and women alike.

Jeanne Garane, University of South Carolina, Columbia

Bibliography

Almeida, Irène Assiba d'. *Francophone Women Writers: Destroying the Emptiness of Silence.* Gainesville: University P of Florida, 1994.

Bâ, Sylvia Washington. *The Concept of Negritude in the Poetry of Léopold Sédar Senghor.* Princeton: Princeton U P, 1973.

Boyce Davies, Carole. *Black Women, Writing, and Identity: Migrations of the Subject.* London and New York: Routledge, 1994.

Cazenave, Odile. *Femmes rebelles: naissance d'un nouveau roman africain au féminin.* Paris: L'Harmattan, 1996.

Ereneville, Anette Mbaye d'. *Poèmes africains.* Dakar: Centre national d'art français, 1965.

Nwapa, Flora. *Efuru.* (1966) London: Heinemann, 1978.

Ogot, Grace. *The Promised Land.* (1966) Nairobi: East African Publishing House, 1974.

Stratton, Florence. *Contemporary African Literature and the Politics of Gender.* London and New York: Routledge, 1994.

Washington, Mary Helen. "Plain, Black, and Decently Wild." *The Voyage In: Fictions of Female Development.* Eds. Elizabeth Abel, Marianne Hirsch, and Elizabeth Langland. Hanover and London: University P of New England, 1983. 270-286.

Preface

I became interested in African literature during a class taught by Senegalese novelist Aminata Sow-Fall at the University of South Carolina, Columbia in the Fall semester of 1997. The next year I continued my studies of Francophone African literature with Professor Jeanne Garane and shortly thereafter I began studying Anglophone African literature with Professor Kwame Dawes. The more I was exposed to African literature, in French or in English, and the characters who inhabited the pages of those novels, the more fascinated I found notions of self-development or *Bildung*, especially in an African Post-Colonial context. On a related level and adding even more to the richness of the analytical endeavor, I came to realize that the authors of these novels, too, have experienced remarkable individuation some of which makes its way, slightly veiled, into the novels themselves. How can Africans, having dealt with complex power relationships because of the influence of Western culture in their own country during Colonization, succeed at self-development? How is it possible ultimately to escape the control of the colonizers and become one's own person? More importantly, and the clear concern of this book, can African female characters ever hope to arrive at such individuation given the multiple challenges they must take on, namely the power structures defined and enforced by European colonizers as well as the patriarchal structures which contort issues related to gender? The concept of *Bildungsroman* or novel of self-development has been around for more than two centuries and much has been researched and written concerning the genre since Geothe's proto-typical novel *Wilhelm Meisters Lehrjahre* appeared in 1795. While feminist critics have analyzed the possibilities and potentials for the individuation of mostly Western, mostly European female characters, this book extends the investigation further by examining the possibilities for self-development for African female protagonists in five selected novels by African female novelists Buchi Emecheta, Tsitsi Dangarembga and Calixthe Beyala.

> Walter P. Collins, III
> University of South Carolina, Lancaster
> Autumn 2005

Acknowledgements

I would like to thank my former professors at the University of South Carolina, Columbia who introduced me to Anglophone and Francophone Post-Colonial African Literature and Theory: Dr. Kwame Dawes, Dr. Jeanne Garane and Dr. Allen Miller. Thanks also to Dr. Nancy Lance for her insight and constructive criticism. In addition, I would like to thank Dean John Catalano, University of South Carolina, Lancaster, for his support and leadership. Ultimately, I thank my wife, Ashley, and my son, Jack, for their love and encouragement.

Permission has been granted to quote from Marjolijn de Jager's English translation of Calixthe Beyala's *Loukoum: The Little Prince of Belleville* by the translator.

Permission has been granted to quote from Calixthe Beyala's *Maman a un amant* by Éditions Albin Michel:
> "Maman a un amant" de Calixthe Beyala
> © Editions Albin Michel S.A., 1993

Permission has been granted to quote from Buchi Emecheta's *In the Ditch* by Heinemann Publishers, Ltd.

Introduction

> "*In his autobiography Goethe stresses the freedom necessary for human development and views personal cultivation as a continuing project of the highest ethical significance: Auf eigene moralische Bildung loszuarbeiten, ist das Einfachste und Tulichste, was der Mensch vornehmen Kann [To go to work on one's own moral Bildung is the simplest and most advisable thing that a person can do].*" —Todd Kontje

This book undertakes an examination of the development of the post-colonial self, more specifically the post-colonial female self as featured in *Second Class Citizen* (1974) and *In the Ditch* (1972) by Nigerian novelist Buchi Emecheta, *Nervous Conditions* (1988) by Zimbabwean novelist Tsitsi Dangarembga, and *Le petit prince de Belleville* (1992) and *Maman a un amant* (1993) by Cameroonian novelist Calixthe Beyala. Each of these texts focuses on a central protagonist who undergoes qualified development and individuation, subversive changes in post-colonial and patriarchal contexts. Reading late twentieth-century Nigerian, Zimbabwean, and Cameroonian texts as modern *Bildungsromane* exposes the dynamics, complexities, and challenges the characters and their authors experience. Before moving forward with an analysis of these five recent African texts, texts wherein characters undergo their own particular *Bildungsprozess* in the context of their own life situation as well as colonization and necessary displacement which has them living in or at close proximity to Western influence, it will be necessary to trace the genesis and history of this genre. In so doing, it will also be necessary to come to an understanding of how this primarily nineteenth-century, Western, and, according to many critics, sexist genre has been used more recently to interpret feminist and post-colonial African literature.

One cannot get far into a serious study of the European novel of the last two and a half centuries without encountering the German literary category *Bildungsroman*. Often used and misused, the term peppers literary discussions untranslated and frequently not fully understood. Scholars such as Frederick Amrine, R. Hinton Thomas, Jeffrey L. Sammons, Franco Moretti, Rita Felski, and Marianne Hirsch have spent years trying to untangle and sort out the history, theory, essence, and application of this novel of development, formation, and education. Likewise, these and others too have focused concern on this critical literary term itself, which is employed too often haphazardly and problematically. Oversimplification and overgeneralization are perhaps to blame for most of the problems surrounding the use of the term *Bildungsroman*.

Jeffrey L. Sammons recounts the telling incident of finding the term on a "Word of the Day" vocabulary building calendar he had bought for his children. Exemplary of the kinds of hermeneutical problems one faces when dealing with *Bildungsromane*, the calendar "defined [the term] thus: 'a novel about the moral and psychological growth of the main character.' There followed," continues Sammons, "an illustrative example: 'D. H. Lawrence's 'Sons and Lovers' is a *bildungsroman* with a heavily autobiographical content'" (26). Sammons immediately points out the irony in using a British novel as an example of a German literary term and literary genre. But perhaps more importantly, even though his children did not or in fact most adults would not linger deep in thought that day to challenge the accuracy of either the definition or the example, Sammons questions the utility of the calendar's nugget of knowledge "for serious discourse about literature" (26). While acknowledging that defining the various terms *dactyl, iamb,* or even *sonnet* is generally non-problematic, Sammons warns that precision with definitions for literary periods and genres is much trickier because the process involves "the insecurities of historiography in general [which] are not infrequently freighted with ideology" (27). The elusiveness of the term combined with the difficulty of locating a good number of specific and individual novels that fit a given definition of the genre have led to some rather far-fetched and even radical pronouncements.

Because the exact defining characteristics of the *Bildungsroman* have been difficult to make precise, critics debate novels they believe to be exemplary of the genre's definition *du jour*. Interestingly, in one instance, Sammons has been bold enough to find the *Bildungsroman* a "myth" and "missing" ("Mystery"). How brazen a claim given that so many scholars over more than two centuries have pinpointed the origin of the genre to the late-eighteenth century and recognized Johann Wolfgang Goethe's *Wilhelm Meisters Lehrjahre* (1795) as the prototype novel. Nevertheless, Sammons relates that there did not exist a single book devoted wholly to the genre in the nineteenth century until 1972 and, although critical discussion on the notion of *Bildungsroman* was certainly circulating, "it communicated a conflicted and diffuse scholarly situation" ("Mystery" 239). Trying to untangle the disorienting mess himself, Sammons set out to find and read the various volumes categorized as *Bildungsromane*. He reports that he not only had difficulty finding the novels, but what is worse, he was unable to find anyone who could definitively identify the titles. Where then does this lead (or leave) us? What of all the extant "conflicted and diffuse" scholarship? Does this genre exist or is it a phantom genre? How do we arrive at a useful definition applicable to a genre of literature reputed to span parts of three centuries? At the end of his chapter in James Hardin's collection of essays, Sammons declares:

I think that the Bildungsroman should have something to do with *Bildung*, that is, with the early bourgeois, humanistic concept of the shaping of the individual self from its innate potentialities through acculturation and social experience to the threshold of maturity....It does not matter whether the process of *Bildung* succeeds or fails, whether the protagonist achieves an accommodation with life and society or not....But *Bildung* is not merely the accumulation of experience, not merely maturation in the form of fictional biography. There must be a sense of evolutionary change within the self, a teleology of individuality, even if the novel, as many do, comes to doubt or deny the possibility of achieving a gratifying result. Certainly the Bildungsroman can be treated as an ideal type that does not necessarily have to be in contact with the German novel tradition or the *Humanitätsphilosophie* of the age of Goethe or Humboldt. (41)

With the ultimate intention of discovering the whereabouts, status, and function of today's *Bildungsroman*, assuming it does exist, we are obliged to consider not only European literature of the late eighteenth, nineteenth and twentieth centuries, but also the general social, economic, and historical tenor of these years.

Chapter 1

The Essence of the *Bildungsroman*: History and Theory, Possibilities and Future

Genesis and History of a New Type of Novel

Selfhood and its formation have, since the reflective individual first set pen to paper, been intriguing and complex notions. The determination of who one is, what one's place is in society and the world, and how one interacts with other selves involves much examination and contemplation. Without question Augustine, Thomas More, Montaigne, Descartes, Spinoza, Rousseau, Kant, Wollstonecraft, Schopenhauer, Hegel, Taylor and many others were occupied with determinations of selfhood and interrelationships between social beings. Yet these thinkers are all Westerners and have contributed to a conception of individuality quite divergent from that present in African literature. African novels deal with perhaps even more complex conceptions of selfhood and notions of relationship of self to society. For instance, Oyekan Owomoyela in his *African Literatures: An Introduction*, highlights the notion of selfhood and other distin-

guishing characteristics in what sounds much like an apologia for African literature. By way of background, Owomoyela writes that African novels were often
criticized from the beginning by Western readers for seemingly one-dimensional
characters; characters who are approached "objectively, [with descriptions of]
their external reactions to their circumstances without attempting to probe their
minds in order to illuminate the psychological forces that motivate their actions"
(*African Literatures* 77). However, he posits that if the African novel "is to be
indistinguishable from the Western in every particular, then these stylistic devia-
tions certainly constitute flaws" (77). Fortunately, he argues that a direct correspondence in terms of qualities need not be necessary; in other words, the Western novel was not the standard by which African literature is to be evaluated.
Owomoyela then reminds readers that African society is intrinsically communal.
"Because the African is expected to be motivated communally," he says, " . . .
interest in individual motivations is out of place because it would assume an
individualism that is actually nonexistent except as an aberration" (80). Likewise,
oncerning two prominent African writers, Katherine Fishburn adds:

> Because we start from a philosophical premise that valorizes indi-
> vidualism, while remaining deeply skeptical of society, we Western
> readers come to these women's [Mariama Bâ and Buchi Emecheta]
> texts ill-prepared to understand them. If we hope to understand this
> literature, then, we must at the very least acknowledge intellectually
> (if not emotionally) that there is more than one way to conceptualize
> the relationship between an individual and society. We must be will-
> ing to accept the fact that societies are not by definition harmful or
> hostile to individuals, that indeed individuals can be inseparable from
> their societies. (37)

In general, African novels offer a much more flexible perspective on the relationship between the individual and society. In most cases, the development of
the individual in African literature and the continuation of communal ways of
life are not at odds. Chinua Achebe's *Things Fall Apart* offers an excellent example of such a text in that Okonkwo faces the challenges of balancing his personal objectives aimed at individual greatness with his responsibilities to the
community in which he resides. While Okonkwo is unsuccessful and the text
ends with his suicide, the interconnectedness of two seemingly disparate areas
remains apparent. On the contrary, Western texts generally champion the individual while offering harsh critiques of society.

   The dawning of the Age of Reason and Enlightenment, the rippling effects
through the social consciousness of multiple countries triggered by the French
Revolution, and the almost simultaneous advent of the modern novel combined
with movements like *Sturm und Drang*[1], fueled and intensified interest in the
formation of the self and selfhood. The German *Bildungsroman*, a new kind of
genre appearing at the close of the eighteenth century with its preoccupation for
tracing self-formation, is undoubtedly a literary outgrowth of the social, economic, philosophical, and historical manifestations of its time. It is critical to

note, however, that the late-eighteenth century developing notion of *Bildung* unveiled a broader application of development and selfhood than ever before. Dennis Mahoney remarks that while the term *Bildung* was soon used regularly in conjunction with the terms *Erziehung* (education) and *Aufklärung* (enlightenment), the process of *Bildung* involved much more than instruction from teachers or mentors (109). Mahoney insists too that "in contrast to the more reason-oriented concept of enlightenment, Bildung was understood as affecting the entire human being—mind, body, and spirit" (109). The notion of *Bildung* must be understood as a progressive and dynamic development not only because it transforms the way individuals view themselves, but also for the promise it extends to the future of extended prose fiction.

In her book-length study entitled *Wilhelm Meister and his English Kinsmen: Apprentices to Life* (1930), Susanne Howe relates that the "*Bildungsroman* [. . .] was in no sense a German invention, but a German reshaping of eighteenth-century ideas current in Europe but well steeped in German atmosphere, and growing gradually into a fiction form particularly congenial to German taste" (24). Individuals and their interactions with others and the world have always been good material for telling stories, reminds Howe (1). She further explains:

> It seems that, long before men's minds began to work in capitals on such antitheses [man and the world], the latent story material in the subject appealed to the eager author, perhaps because it implied the gaining of experience—usually the author's own—at the hands of the world, and therefore it involved action, travel. . . . After all—putting aside for the moment Miss Austen's *Emma* and a few other magnificent exceptions—no one can learn much of anything at home. Going somewhere is the thing. And there—in all sorts of tempting variety— is your story. (1)

While narratives of development and apprenticeship to life of a similar ilk as the *Bildungsroman* undoubtedly existed before *Wilhelm Meisters Lehrjahre*, Goethe's landmark novel became the original model, by tying together a variety of loose ends, which future novels of development would emulate as well as variegate.

The necessity of defamiliarizing oneself with one's native surroundings as well as other aspects characteristic of Goethe's hero and narrative were already in practice before the publication the *Lehrjahre*. For example, Howe cites elements of epic-like travel replete with characters' exposure to worldly ways and "profound shocks" in Voltaire's story *Candide* (1759) (2-3). She also mentions "novels of youth," typically of English or German extraction, wherein the

> adolescent hero of the typical 'apprentice' novel sets out on his way through the world, meets with reverses usually due to his own tem-

perament, falls in with various guides and counsellors, makes many
false starts in choosing his friends, his wife, and his life work, and finally adjusts himself in some way to the demands of his time and environment by finding a sphere of action in which he may work effec-
tively[2]. (4)

Similarly, she finds clear and inherent filiation in the hero of the *Bildungsroman*
with the "recalcitrant hero" of the moral allegory who, during his ramblings,
faces representations, often in human form, of both good and bad and from
whom he must learn, out-smart, or perhaps receive temporary defeat (5). Howe,
along with other scholars, also places the hero of the *Bildungsroman* on the
same family tree with picaresque heroes like the protagonists from *Francion*
(1623), *Gil Blas* (1735), and *Tom Jones* (1749) (5). In addition, she sees connections to the "universal man" of the Renaissance who is "bent on developing all
his gifts to the utmost and welding them into an artistic whole" (5). Other
movements and characteristics influencing the development of the *Bildungsroman* include Pietism[3] and the confessional style of writing practiced by Jean-
Jacques Rousseau, and later by Thomas Carlyle, George Meredith, and, in some
senses, by Lord Byron (Howe 6-9).

It is important to understand the transformation in German literary output of
the late-eighteenth century both in terms of quality and quantity. The world of
German literature prior to the 1780s had little or nothing of which to boast.
While her neighboring countries of France, Spain, and England could claim accomplished writers and established literary traditions, Germany's writers strug-
gled to produce much of any significance. Three writers, Opitz in the seventeenth century and Gotthold Ephraim Lessing and Christoph Martin Wieland in
the eighteenth century, were well versed in the literature of peer aspirants of
varying nationalities and sought to create for Germany a national standard for
literature with all the richness and depth of French, Spanish, and English texts.
T. J. Reed recounts that the latter two authors/critics took the first real steps in
propelling German literature toward a brighter future:

> Wieland and Lessing did what was possible in this 'Zeit der
> deutschen Nichtliteratur', as it was later called. Wieland practiced a
> gentle criticism and a gradual inculcation of stylistic elegance. Less-
> ing was more uncompromising. With his clear-sighted critical cam-
> paigns and robust creativity he had the largest part in initiating what
> is usually called the 'literary revival' in eighteenth-century Germany.
> (11)

The novel that in many ways is a clear forerunner to the *Bildungsroman* was
Wieland's *Die Geschichte des Agathon*. This novel, according to Christian Friedrich von Blanckenburg, author of *Versuch über den Roman* [*Essay on the
Novel*, 1774] and the first German apologist of the novel, demonstrates a unity
"by portraying Agathon's inner development in strict accordance with the laws
of causality" (Kontje 8). Within the first few chapters, Agathon experiences nu-

merous events from being abducted by pirates to being seduced by a famous courtesan. Most significantly, readers get immediate and vivid insight into Agathon's thoughts and concerns regarding his exploits. Kontje concludes that "[by] emphasizing Wieland's concentration on the psychological development of one central protagonist, Blanckenburg identifies the beginning of a German novel tradition that will come to be called the Bildungsroman" (8). While most of Blanckenburg's comments in *Versuch über den Roman* are not particularly original or even directed towards novels (many examples are instead taken from drama), scholars tend to agree that his comments on *Die Geschichte des Agathon* represent some of his most original. If Wieland and Lessing brought about revival in German literature; most scholars, including Reed, would contend that Goethe ushered in a literary renaissance. (12). Goethe's early work such as *Die Leiden des jungen Werther* of 1774 and his drama "Götz von Berlichingen" presented "a quality [of literature] which Germany had not seen since the Middle Ages" (Reed 12). Goethe's contributions to Germany's literary upswing, especially with the publication of *Wilhelm Meister*, cannot be exaggerated or overstated.

Citing Max Wundt's insightful early twentieth century study[4] of Goethe's *Wilhelm Meister*, Randolph P. Shaffner catalogues qualities that Goethe's publication crystalized. He writes: "in his chapter on the novel of the eighteenth century [Wundt] concludes that the apprenticeship novel, on the crest of a wave of contemporaneous tendencies, united 'all the otherwise separate types of the novel'" (7). According to Wundt, the most important pre-existing traits that the apprenticeship novel inherited and brought together were:

> 'the focus on the inner life,' which relates it to the novel of sentiment; itself an outgrowth of the romantic novel, the 'Liebesroman'; 'the striving for knowledge of the world' of the novel of travel, itself a later development of the novel of adventure; 'the critical attitude toward the world' of the satirical novel; the 'presentation of individual development' of the psychological and the biographical novels; and the 'colorful portrayal of life and the world' of the broader novel of culture. (qtd. in Shaffner 7)

The birthplace of the prototypical *Bildungsroman, Wilhelm Meisters Lehrjarhe*, not only coincides with a socio-historical period of heightened interest in individual self-identity and self-conception, but also constitutes the intersection of several types of novelistic trends existing separately before it.

During the second half of the eighteenth century, the novel came to be considered primarily the "literature" of the populace. Reed acknowledges that "[the novel] had been prominent on the publishing, if not the literary scene since the mid-[eighteenth] century; [and that it was] produced in ever growing numbers for a voracious public" (98). Growing ubiquity, however, did not guarantee quality. Reed draws an analogy with one of the twenty-first century's favorite pastimes: "Popularity usually inspires suspicion; the novel was the television of the eighteenth century" (98). In 1774, Blanckenburg, in his aforementioned *Essay on the Novel*, came to the rescue by praising the novel and by alluding to its potential power because more people than ever before now had access to it. Furthermore, Blanckenburg hints that the novel could be for modern times, what the epic had been for the Greeks (Reed 99). In 1795, Blanckenburg's suggestion was legitimized by Hegel when in his *Ästhetik* he "accepts the novel without question as the modern form of the epic, 'die moderne bürgerliche Epopöe'. . ." (Reed 100). For decades, the terms "novel" and "roman" brought immediate suggestions of the banal and the quotidian. Such associations were fueled partly by the sheer number of novels published in the late 1700s—"one bookseller put the production of novels, German and translated, at three hundred a year in the 1790s and at nearly six thousand for the span 1773 to 1794" (Reed 100). A second challenge to the novel's full acceptance as a bonafide genre stemmed from an inability, if not outright refusal, by those in the literary world to reconcile the conflict between poetry and prosaic reality (Reed 100). But with the publication of *Wilhelm Meister* and subsequent to Hegel's proclamation in *Ästhetik*, a change in perception of this new genre began. Reed observes that "[just as *Wilhelm Meister's*] subject matter makes it a history of the various kinds of culture coexisting in eighteenth century Germany—bourgeois, noble, Enlightened, pietist, bohemian—so its treatment makes it a compendium of the literary means and motifs which were to be found in novels high and low and in other works which fed the new genre" (101). Goethe's work was the spark that would eventually illuminate what is perhaps considered Germany's most renowned literary period.

Until 1961, when Fritz Martini proved otherwise, most scholars believed that it was Wilhelm Dilthey in his 1870 biography of Friedrich Schleiermacher who first used the term *Bildungsroman*. Martini found evidence demonstrating that Karl Morgenstern, professor of rhetoric in what is now modern day Estonia, used the term as early as 1803. Furthermore, between 1817 and 1824, Morgenstern had also published three more essays on the *Bildungsroman*. Not only had a new literary term been coined earlier than previously thought, but also a transformation in meaning of the term *Bildung* was underway.

The term *Bildung* underwent a shift in meaning in the late 1700s and early 1800s with progressive development of various concepts of individuality and with the rise of this new type of novel. Todd Kontje recalls that the notion of *Bildung* finds its roots in spiritual or religious realms (2-3). The contemporary interpretation of *Bildung* came about through a radical redefining process propelled by the work of Johann Gottfried Herder that took place near the end of the eighteenth century. The term underwent a shift in definition morphing from the long held concept of divine shaping and forming to individual formation through personal interaction—in other words, from "God's active transformation of the passive Christian" to a new interpretation imbued with environmental determinism and cultural relativism (Kontje 1-2). In his *Ideen zur Philosophie der Geschichte der Menschheit* (1784-91), Herder, while attempting to write the history of the world and its people groups, "insists that all human beings are part of the same species, but that different 'climates' produce cultural differences between peoples" (2). As he discusses the history of peoples of the world in his work, Herder reminds that one should not be overly critical of people groups of former times and far away places. Different environments and experiences have caused them to become different individuals. Interestingly enough, Kontje sets forth Herder's decisive condemnation of European colonialism noting the hypocrisy of the project—the Europeans, writes the critic, "have abolished slavery at home only to enslave the world in a misguided attempt to annihilate cultural differences" (3). According to Kontje, Herder's "teleological narrative" critiques the way individuals and things were, the way they are, all the while inscribing an "exhortation to his own people to become what they ought to be" (3). The nineteenth century, Kontje remarks, witnesses a similar impelling force as critical minds prod writers to continually improve the German novel (3). Since Herder's work in the late 1700s, interested scholars of eighteenth, nineteenth, and twentieth-century literature, both Germanists and others, have consistently written, thought and theorized about the *Bildungsroman* from numerous perspectives and directions.

The Weimar Classicists

The work of one particular group, the Weimar Classicists, composed principally of Goethe, and J. C. Frederich von Schiller, but also of G. E. Lessing, Wieland, and Wilhelm von Humboldt, focused on the burgeoning and evolving notion of *Bildung* as they promoted a new aestheticism for German literature. Changing readers' understanding and preconceived conceptions of literature's direction was indeed a slow and tedious task. Klaus L. Berghahn asserts that "one should take care not to imagine Weimar Classicism as a harmonic, restful epoch triumphantly closing a period that had seen the blossoming of German literature. It would be wiser to represent German literature in that period as being in a state of development and still controversial" (85). Controversial indeed primarily because of new theories of art and aesthetics set forth by Schiller and Goethe.

The Kant-influenced theories of J. C. Frederich von Schiller center on the formation of a perfect society wherein there exists not only an aesthetic balance in and of itself " to reproduce the whole human being within us," but also an established standard set high to be reached by the best poets (Berghahn 79). The works of these poets would speak to the masses; the poets would be there to see that the process, this unification of the public, is successful. In Schiller's mind, "the critic no longer speaks on behalf of a general public, and certainly not for the 'people,' but for a literary elite. However, this group [of poets] is not to shut itself off in an elitist fashion; rather, as 'spokesmen for the people's feelings,' its members should lower themselves to the people's level in order to 'laughingly and playfully draw it up to their level'" (Berghahn 79-80). Ramifications of such a shift in mindset produced sweeping changes in the way art and literature were received. Among such changes, Berghahn cites these:

> criticism is uncoupled from reception; the artwork possesses an abso-
> lute value, one existing independent of the readers' ability to com-
> prehend it intellectually. The critic examines only whether a work
> corresponds to "the highest demands of art," not whether it is gener-
> ally pleasing. Art becomes autonomous, and the critic defends it
> against the leveling taste of the public. (80)

Schiller's aesthetic theories unmistakably have an elitist bent, yet they have proven useful and enduring over the years. Schiller's contributions to the idea of *Bildung* are seemingly less direct because they are philosophically more complex and ethereal than those of other writers and critics like Wieland and Goethe. Nonetheless, the novel notions of late-eighteenth century Schillerian aesthetics led ultimately, if not directly, to transformations in sensibilities, ways of perceiving art and literature, and most importantly the behavior of individuals. All of these changes comprise in turn the *Bildungsprozess* believed to be necessary for growth, development, and self-expansion of not only the character used in a text, but also perhaps, of the reader of the text[5]. The Weimar Classicists generated new ideas, new formulations of what literature is as they issued a steady and unrelenting challenge to bring to life literature worthy and capable of uniting Germany by embodying a national spirit.

Approximately twenty years before the appearance of *Wilhelm Meister*, Goethe drew a large audience after the publication of *Werther*. The subject matter of the novel coupled with its depiction and defense of suicide captivated young readers in particular. Yet it must be recalled, as discussed earlier, that in the 1770s the novel was still by and large a genre for the general population. With the publication of *Wilhelm Meister*, Kontje suggests that "the nascent split between the popular novel and a select number of demanding works becomes particularly evident" (9). *Wilhelm Meister* indeed led in a new direction, as it required much more of its readers than literature really ever had before. Although critics like Schiller, Gottfried Körner, Friedrich Schlegel, and Novalis never used the term *Bildungsroman*, they knew that something new was happening. This novel was of great significance for the future of German literature.

More than any other writer or critic during the late-eighteenth and early nineteenth centuries, it is Goethe who is credited with shaping the sweeping changes that would launch not only significant German literature, but also the modern novel—a fledgling genre replete with dynamic intrigue and with characters of a depth and roundness rarely seen before. In point of fact, Georg Lukács offers this summation of Goethe's evolving narrative abilities:

[Goethe] concentrates the action upon a few dramatic scenes and achieves a close connection between figures and events. This was later offered by Balzac as a characteristic difference between modern fiction and that of the seventeenth and eighteenth century. If we compare the manner in which Goethe introduces figures such as Philine and Mignon in *Theatralische Sendung*[6] and in [*Wilhelm Meisters*] *Lehrjahre* we can easily recognize this "dramatic" purpose; it is no mere technical shift: some of the figures are now richer and more complex and have a greater psychological range and tension. . . . Figures like Philine and Mignon who achieve emotional presence and vitality with the most economical artistic skill, are unique in world literature. (96-97)

Goethe's writing found inspiration in his surroundings. Historically speaking, Europe was pulling away from the outdated feudal system as middle class and bourgeois notions were forming. Individuals aggressively sought their own autonomy as they "turned almost simultaneously against past orthodoxy and the coming economic, technical, and political revolutions" (Lange 2). But critics agree that what made Goethe such a notable writer, intellectual, and forger of change was his ability to observe carefully and interact wisely with his surroundings. According to Victor Lange, "What distinguishes him from a host of remarkable contemporaries is his readiness, from youth to old age, to draw the world about him into his constantly receptive, unceasingly active and reflective mind" (3). It is critical to note that Goethe was not only uncommonly receptive and reflective, but he was indeed inventive and innovative.

The revealing correspondence between Schiller and Goethe is well documented and provides singular perspectives into the creation in particular of *Wilhelm Meisters Lehrjahre*. From December 1794 through the summer of 1796, Goethe sent Schiller manuscripts of various sections of the text. Schiller's reception of the text is positive and at first, relates Kontje, he offers "only cautious suggestions for minor revisions. Increasingly, however, he [Schiller] displays impatience with what he feels is Goethe's unwillingness to express more clearly 'die Idee des Ganzen,' the single concept that unifies the whole (10). Schiller, himself a dramatist, maintained many reservations concerning narrative fiction. According to Lange, Schiller sought to convince Goethe that more attention should be given to philosophical aspects of Wilhelm's growth and formation (75). Yet this was exactly what Goethe sought to avoid—"he knew and had read with little enthusiasm Klinger's philosophical novels, he was not much interested in Jacobi's *Allwill*, and he had barely commented upon Wieland's *Agathon*—all works with an explicit philosophical purpose and little poetic resonance" (Lange 75). Goethe was convinced that his project would break new ground. He was well aware of the shortcomings of *Theatralische Sendung*— Lange calls it "a specimen of satirical portraiture"—and worked diligently to make *Wilhelm Meister* quite different (76). Schiller's insistence that Goethe express more clearly a unifying concept as well as other Schillerian notions eventually prompts Goethe to end his dialogue with Schiller and send his manuscript to press without further collaboration.

Many easily forget that Goethe was quite enamored with science or what was then termed natural philosophy. Nevertheless, most critics now consider his work in science to be foundational to his literary exploits. Lange observes that his "scientific interest sustained his thinking and his writing and gave coherence and meaning to what might otherwise have been merely an effervescent romantic genius" (3). While this is certainly true, Lange continues by noting that "it is obvious that his notion of science was not, in the modern sense, objective, specific, and delimiting: his purpose in dealing with natural phenomena was to discover models that would satisfy his curiosity as to the principles of functioning, of relationships, of interdependence" (3). Through all of this, Goethe embraced the expanding notion of *Bildung* and studied its application to organic matter such as seeds. He wrote *Die Metamorphose der Pflanzen* [*The Metamorphosis of Plants*] in 1799 and *Metamorphose der Tiere* [*Metamorphosis of Animals*] twenty-one years later. Goethe also saw in science examples of cohesion and continuity that were certainly applicable to those he examined in his literature. Lange clarifies succinctly Goethe's position on science and its extensive applications to other areas in the following manner:

> For science . . . must serve the human obligation not to impose abstractly, but to discover empirically, the forms by which life in its totality can be understood and ordered. Form and substance were, therefore, in his [Goethe's] morphological thinking, aspects of the same phenomenon; throughout his work, whether scientific or literary, he argued this unity of substance and form and the capacity of the imagination to serve as the instrument by which we articulate the shape and structure of the world about us. (4)

This perspective on form and substance, products of complete allegiance to scientific empiricism, indeed serves as Goethe's defining characteristic and made his literature, especially *Wilhelm Meister*, unique. He did not feel the need to follow conceptual schemas of others [Kant or Hegel], notes Lange; instead, "[history,] whether of individuals or civilizations, was for him the tangible sum of available forms of experience; to find and achieve form, to demonstrate it as the instrument of truth, seemed to [Goethe] the natural purpose of a responsible life" (4). Included in this responsible life, the life of the writer/revealer and the lives of his exemplary characters, and in fact underlying squarely and infused within all of Goethe's understanding of an individual's purpose is the notion of the *Bildungprozess*. Kontje reminds us that in his autobiography Goethe "stresses the freedom necessary for human development and views personal cultivation as a continuing project of the highest ethical significance: 'to go to work on one's own moral *Bildung* is the simplest and most advisable thing that a person can do'" (4). Goethe's theories of *Bildung* continue to inspire and to influence writers and thinkers into the nineteenth century and well beyond.

Social, Historical, and Political Influences

The French Revolution served as but a hint of the political and social unrest to come as both liberal and conservative factions in and around Germany continuously interacted and fought for their own agendas well into the nineteenth century. After Napoleon's defeat in 1815, German politics witnessed a quick turn to conservatism. Yet, all the while, undercurrents of liberal ideologies were developing. The region's leaders worked hard to keep a handle on what were perceived by them as radical new ideas. Kontje acknowledges that "[the] governments [of Germany, the Austro-Hungarian Empire, and Prussia] reacted consistently with attempts to suppress dissidence, beginning with the Draconian Carlsbad Decrees of 1819 and continuing with the official ban on the publications of the radical Young Germans in 1835, until the quick collapse of the disorganized Frankfurt Parliament brought the restoration of conservative rule (13-4). Despite political and social instability, the first half of the nineteenth century brought increased literacy and publication. Nevertheless, the novel as a genre was for many years still too new to be accepted as anything more than "aesthetically careless and morally dangerous" (Kontje 14).

The literary critics of the early nineteenth century were a surprising bunch. As traditional academic critics did not speak out about or promote the genre, groups like the Young Germans, politically progressive and democratic in ideology, took up the task of helping all levels of society understand the novel. Hartmut Steinecke contends that "[we] must look elsewhere when seeking significant contributions to the study of the novel during the period [early-nineteenth century], namely to publications that are not conceived as aesthetic theory in the narrower sense of the term. These publications include prefaces, newspaper articles, contributions to reference works, and book reviews" (qtd. in Kontje 14). Georg Herwegh and Ludwig Börne, critics who promoted political reform through literary accessibility and understanding, wanted individuals to have equal access not only to literature and its criticism, but also to benefit from what Peter Uwe Hohendahl suggests as "a democratization of the public sphere" (qtd. in Kontje 14). As critics promoted literary works and ideas from their end, writers continued to publish novels—novels of development certainly, but also novels that would transform the romantic *Bildungsroman* à la Goethe into novels of development more befitting the times in which they were written.

Moving Beyond Goethe

Even as early as 1815, writes Kontje, the novel began to turn away from the model romantic *Bildungsroman* of the late-eighteenth century. In Joseph Freiherr von Eichendorff's *Ahnung und Gegenwart* [*Presentiment and Presence of*

1815], the central protagonist, Friedrich, faces a jolting reality when he "rejects [the] decadent society to become a heroic soldier in the struggle against Napoleon. In the end he renounces the world entirely and becomes a monk" (Kontje 15). Broader perspectives and real life history invade the genre of the novel as the individual, at this period more than ever, contends with his place in society. Similarly, there exists a question of one's place in the greater society in E. T. A. Hoffmann's *Lebens-Ansichten des Katers Murr* [*The Life and Opinions of Tomcat Murr*]. Written from 1819-1821, Hoffmann's novel is to be read as satire and functions as a forum for critique of the government and of social status. The story relates tales of a frolicking cat and is the thinly veiled, but turbulent life story of musician Johannes Kreisler complete with a "corrupt provincial court [which] serves as a metaphor for Metternich's Europe" (Kontje 15). Again the notion of the larger society figures predominantly in the novel. Finally, Karl Leberecht Immermann's *Die Epigonen* of 1836 is perhaps the most successful attempt at updating Goethe's masterpiece. "Immermann's concentration on the development of a single protagonist reflects the influence of Goethe's *Lehrjahre* . . . ,[but] Immermann uses the novel to address such contemporary issues as political radicalism, the fate of the aristocracy, and the rise of industrialism" (Kontje 20). From the 1820s through the 1840s, novels from neighboring European countries brought new ideas and novelistic formats to Germany. Kontje points out that the novels of Honoré Balzac, George Sand, and Eugène Sue occupied the thoughts and conversations of literary critics, especially in the 1830s and '40s (15).

Perhaps the most influential publications in the 1820s were Walter Scott's historical novels that prompted many German writers to try their hand at such narrative. Real life had grown too dynamic to ignore and according to Steinecke, the new fascination with the historical novel triggered a change in direction away from the idealism of the past toward the realities of the contemporary world (50). Passé were the tales of heroism with their hint of aristocratic flamboyance; these were the days, concludes Wolfgang Menzel, of novels of the people and of democracy (Kontje 19). Despite this advancement, in ideology and practice, Germany always seemed to be at least one step behind her French and English neighbors. She dealt with a lack of political unity and interminable snarls while developing a literary identity; two completely interrelated phenomena. Berthold Auerbach offered one suggestion to help solve some of the country's problems. His proposition sought "to effect change through literature that extended the possibility of *Bildung* to a broader segment of society" (Kontje 21). In 1845, this concept was also taken up by Robert Prutz in his essay *Über die Unterhaltungsliteratur, insbesondere der Deutschen* [*On Popular Literarure, Particularly That of the Germans*]. He maintains that if German literature could reach out to a wider range of people then it would go a long way in aligning itself more with the rest of European literature. "Prutz situates his argument in a philosophy of history that sees the current impoverished age as the inevitable first stage in a process that will lead to a higher level of German culture and— implicitly—to greater political freedom" (Kontje 21). He wants to tap into more popular forms of literature; he believes that "what is good in German literature is boring, and what is entertaining is bad" (Kontje 21). Prutz's goal is that Germany's emergent national literature be both good and entertaining.

Changing Times

By the mid-nineteenth century, France, the United Kingdom, and Germany led Europe in industrialization. The inner workings of society were radically different than they had been little more than fifty years before. In fact, Germany was becoming quite a different place. While a politically unified Germany could not be imagined in the late-eighteenth century, the nineteenth century progressed and industrialization and the colonizing urged grasped German society. Colonialism too was well established and European expansion was at its height. From November 15 1884 to November 26, 1885, the Berlin Conference, led by then German Chancellor Otto von Bismarck, divided the African continent into regions to be administered by European powers. The development of industry and overseas colonies is inextricably linked with literary developments of the times. By 1871, Germany was experiencing political unification bolstered by an increasingly respectable national literature. Kontje writes:

> By this time the German literary canon had become firmly established by literary historians who sought to create a national cultural identity that was to prepare the way for political unification. Once that goal had been attained, the freshly minted canon served to legitimate existing authority. The new government [*Kaiserreich*] put German literature into service for the state and institutionalized its study. Hence, the last decades of the nineteenth century witness the establishment of *Germanistik* as a separate discipline at the universities, the growth of academic publications aimed at a specialized audience, and the substitution of German literature for the classics as the basis for education in the primary and secondary schools. (28)

Additionally, life for individuals was more complex because of work and the general obligations and responsibilities that industrialization engendered. Nineteenth century literature reflects this change as well. Franco Moretti recalls the shift that reverberated through all levels of society:

> In *Wilhelm Meister*, everyday life was a spacious domain where the hero was free to discover what the world had to offer, and to leisurely build his 'personality'. In *The Red and the Black* [1830], this space had become a mire, and what could give a meaning to life—amour-passion, politics—had become alien and hostile to a stifling and somewhat cowardly everydayness. With Balzac things change once more, and each everyday occurrence—expanding a business or find-

ing a job, but also buying boots or greeting a passer-by—is suddenly
a complex and unpredictable event, full of promises, or threats, or at
least surprises. (142)

Moretti cites Fernand Braudel whose study *Afterthoughts on Material Civiliza-*
tion and Capitalism identifies the first half of the nineteenth century as the period wherein the greatest societal changes concerning industrialization took
place. Indeed, this was a period of growing dependence on and influence by
forces [capitalism, cosmopolitanism, colonialism and the new social order] outside "the domain of the everyday" (Moretti 142-143). Moretti examines Sten-
dahl and Pushkin as well as Balzac's *Lost Illusions* [1837] and *Old Goriot*
[1835], in order to demonstrate diachronic changes in the *Bildungsroman*.

A Sampling of French and Russian Versions of the Bildungsroman

A back to back reading of *Wilhelm Meister* and *The Red and the Black* reveals shocking differences in two novels of the genre. Moretti suggests, "The
'great world' can no longer be confined to the story's periphery, in hazy revolutions and bloodless wars, but assaults the 'little world', actively forging the interiority of its new heroes" (75). And this "interiority," continues Moretti, is a
divided one. *Bildungsroman* characters are no longer perfectly harmonized and
crafted individuals who find their way easily, comparatively speaking, to an
autonomous selfhood. Instead, the lives of characters in novels represent the
lives of real people facing the real complexities and dualities of real life. Moretti
conceives Napoleon as the "natural representative of an age in which existence
truly becomes what the *Theory of the Novel* calls 'problematic'" (76). Napoleon
was both a General—a soldier and liberator, but also an Emperor—a despot
sanctioned by the Pope. In literature of the period, characters like Julien Sorel
and Eugene Onegine must likewise deal with this complexity of selfhood. Such
complexity of character certainly adds intrigue, "[but] they are also fascinating
in a more technical sense, from the standpoint of narrative structure. For a con-
tradictory character, placed at the centre of a novel as its hero, must of necessity
make the story unpredictable and gripping: it is a guarantee of narrativity, of
suspense" (Moretti 86). Literature echoed the times as the conclusions of the
newer *Bildungsromane* did not come to a smooth and harmonious end. While
the success of classical *Bildungsromane* hinged on the formation of characters in
a prescribed manner, an overarching organic wholeness of narrative and structure, and simply put, an old fashioned "happy ending," the novels of development by Stendhal, Pushkin and Balzac did not require such and therefore are
seen as reflections of the times in which they were written. Moretti synopsizes in
the following manner:

Much more than in 'progress', this age sees in *contradiction* the hidden essence of history. These are the years in which Hegelian dialectics takes its final shape, and in which Goethe, tackling the theme of historical change, decides to use not one, but two protagonists. . . . But this is not the case in novels contemporaneous with *Faust*, where no heavenly host will come to disentangle Julien's courage from his unscrupulous ambition, or Onegin's lucid intelligence from his destructive indifference. The question, for Pushkin and Stendhal, is not 'how do we separate the angel from the demon?', but rather: 'how do they manage to *live together*?' (86-7)

Indeed, Hegel's philosophy of the novel expressed in his *Lectures on Aesthetics* [1835-38] is quite telling (even though he argued, in *The Philosophy of History*, that Africa had no meaningful history, that it was a place lost in time). Hegel views the novel as a modern, middle-class epic. There is no hope in regaining the attributes of the ancient world and "[r]eality has become prosaic, and poetry is preserved only in the individual hero. Thus the novel portrays the conflict between the 'Poesie des Herzens' [poetry of the heart] and the 'Prosa der Verhältnisse' [prose of the surroundings]" (Kontje 23). Consequently, this new genre continues to evolve in step with changing historical, political, and social forces and its plot and intrigue become more elaborate and less facile and predictable.

While Stendhal and Pushkin's characters contend with the contradictions of history around them in their *Bildungsprozess*, Balzac's characters face the city— Paris—and simultaneously exploding capitalism. Moretti posits that the symbolic center of Paris in the nineteenth century was *la Bourse*—the stock exchange and that "[the] 'marriage of capital and chance', which Balzac celebrates . . . , is as disturbing a union as the one –' bourgeois respectability founded on chance'—indicated by Richard Sennett" (143). Nevertheless, chance and the unbiased ruthlessness of the city, truly not unlike the unpredictable and impartial historical turns of event of Stendhal, direct much of the fictitious balzacian world. Balzac also set out to write the great collection of stories of human behavior and manners—*La Comédie Humaine*. The collection features novels with characters that face social, moral, and philosophical dilemmas while coming to grips with modern society and life, for many of them, in the city. In *Old Goriot*, for instance, it is a question of *parvenir*, or making one's way in society. Moretti contends, however, that this notion is quite slippery:

> 'Parvenir'—fine. But 'where'? Not only are we not told, but it is hinted that the question itself is childish. As with money, the fascination of social mobility is in its boundlessness: it is not a question of reaching 'a' position, no matter how high (Napoleon), but of the possibility to become 'anything.' It is the euphoria of an 'open' society, where everything is relative and changing; hence the somewhat paradoxical need for a catchword as suggestive as it is definite. (131)

Certainly, this idea of "making it" suggests much while revealing hardly anything. Nevertheless, at least one aspect of making it in society seems to be a sure thing. It is certain that characters in novels must now face competition.

The notion of competition is one of Balzac's inventive novelistic additions. Before Balzac, notes Moretti, novels presented a world that seemed simply to be taking its natural course until an individual decided to initiate interaction with it. "Balzac's great innovation lies in shifting the origin of plot from an *individual volition* to a *superindividual mechanism*: the mechanism of *competition*, which with the unification of the national markets, in the first half of the nineteenth century, ceases to be an exception to become the *norm* of social relations" (Moretti 147). In Balzac's Paris, the world writes the narrative, and not only does it write the narrative, but the world also enacts the narrative upon the individual. In *Old Goriot* specifically, characters interact, "fight and devour one another like spiders in a pot" (qtd. in Moretti 147). The *Bildungsprozess* is thus propelled not by a simple decision of a certain character to go out and become successful, but instead by the indeterminable whims of a world of capitalistic inequality, twists and turns, and incessant interpersonal struggles. "[The] narrative of youth is no longer the symbolic form able to 'humanize' the social structure, as in *Wilhelm Meister*, nor, as in *The Red and the Black*, to question its cultural legitimacy. It only acts to magnify the indifferent and inhuman vigour of the modern world, which it reconstructs—as if it were an autopsy—from the wounds inflicted upon the individual" (Moretti 164). Perhaps one final observation will demonstrate further the changes capitalism prompted in *Bildungsroman* fiction.

Moretti asserts that the notion of the work ethic, which is tied clearly to capitalism, is the key characteristic of modern bourgeois culture (164). In other words, those who make their way in society and become successful have learned that hard work more often than not pays off and they are willing to sacrifice to find success. Moretti notes further, "Given that one of the great novelties of capitalism is to make production independent of the immediate satisfaction of need—so that man no longer is 'the measure of all things', as was the case in precapitalist societies—then it seems inevitable that the legitimation of the new order should crystalize around that abstract labour which has become its only recognizable foundation" (164-65). Yet what critics find strange when novels of development are analyzed is that this idea of the work ethic is overturned. Unexpectedly, characters in *Bildungsromane* of the nineteenth century, who are on pathways toward self-development and formation and who are model representatives of a burgeoning middle class, avoid work. "[If] Wilhelm [*Wilhelm Meister*] and Julien [*The Red and the Black*] do not actually reject work, although they do not entrust the meaning of their lives to it, Rastignac [*Old Goriot*] and Lucien [*Lost Illusions*] already try to avoid it as much as possible: Frédéric Moreau [*Sentimental Education*], for his part, abhors it: at home he immediately knocks down a wall to enlarge his *salon* at the expense of his studio" (Moretti 165). If the engagement in work assists in legitimizing the modern bourgeois and work is increasingly devalued in these characters that nonetheless experience personal growth, where then are the abilities to develop and *parvenir* derived?

Moretti posits that their formation comes through the "world of consumption" (165). The desire for things and obtaining things opens a new world of possibilities for growth—"It transforms them from 'needs'—a term which evokes the static image of an always identical reproduction—to 'desires': which imply dynamism, change, novelty" (Moretti 165). Paris then becomes the "capital of the nineteenth century" because there, more than anywhere else in Europe, "money could buy anything" (Moretti 166). As with other aspects mentioned above, consumption too is a societal influence that creeps successively into the *Bildungsroman*. Moretti notes that while Julien is not so much changed by the powers of desire in the city and drawn into a lifestyle of consumption, "Rastignac, Lucien, and Frédéric all come to Paris not knowing who they are nor what they want: it is Paris itself, that immense showcase of new social wealth, that will teach them what it means to desire—to desire everything, at every moment" (166). Indeed, it is Paris, replete with her head spinning array of consumer oriented temptations, whose role is so crucial in the advancement of the development of the individual. Furthermore, the success or failure of the protagonist's attempts at self-development is based either upon his good fortune and good decision-making or his miscalculation and illusion[7] (Moretti 167). But if a given protagonist develops fully in this new world of consumption, does simply "having things" make him so or is "being" some thing more important? Moretti clarifies:

> Fascinated yet perplexed, nineteenth-century mentality hesitated a long while at this new crossroads. It did indeed increasingly entrust the formation of individual identity to the mediation of money—nor could it do otherwise: from *Wilhelm Meister* to Balzac and Flaubert, the history of the *Bildungsroman* itself bears witness to the sudden rise of the new social bond. But if 'having' achieves a prominence unimaginable—only two generations earlier—in the Goethian *Bildungsroman*, nineteenth century culture is still reluctant to entrust to it all the reality of 'being': despite the increasingly lifeless and indefinable features of the latter dimension—from the dynamism and versatility of 'having' something was still missing. (171-72)

It seems the dilemma many individuals in certain modern day capitalistic societies face—that of having everything, yet owning nothing[8]—arises in the mid-nineteenth century and corresponds with the pinnacle of colonialism. Moretti cites pertaining to this the literary examples of *Rameau's Nephew, Faust,* and the "self-estranged spirit" of the *Phenomenology* (172). He even goes so far as to adopt the label "tragedy of the consumer" noting the power money can take on in the development of individuals—"perhaps money cannot buy existence, but its lack, on the other hand, definitely forces one *not* to be. Or in other words, to die" (Moretti 174). Moretti suggests that Flaubert is the first to write such a tragedy in his *Madame Bovary* (1856) (173). *Madame Bovary* and *Sentimental Education* present dilemmas and precarious situations for the developing individual. What looks to be the means to development and growth in society, money, can drive one to a hollow and unfulfilled existence; yet the lack of monetary resources leads ultimately to a similar end. Thankfully, Moretti does not leave us here; instead, with the help of Carl Schmitt and Pierre Bourdieu, he proposes the following explanation:

> But thanks to the ironico-aesthetic attitude, the contradiction disappears: on the one hand, the romanticism of fantasy keeps alive all the possibilities of the surrounding world, and even strengthens them beyond measure; on the other hand, since this is an imaginary space and time, which can be reorganized at will, the individual is not forced into that merry-go-round of real identifications which . . . would leave him exhausted and in a thousand pieces. (176)

In other words, what saves an individual from "the great adventure of self-estrangement" and "psychic and spiritual disintegration" is his or her ability to imagine possibility over reality. The protagonist learns to use daydreams and imagination to balance the realities of the forceful demands of the external world with a personal "self-sufficient cosmos . . . at rest within itself" in the process of development (Moretti 174-76).

As has been discussed above, the first century of the European *Bildungsroman* [late-eighteenth through late-nineteenth centuries] was influenced largely by the great social, political, historical, and economic changes various countries underwent and by their colonial projects overseas. Moretti claims that the continental *Bildungsroman* shifted in narrative style and structure as well as preoccupation of subject matter in step with the changing times (181). However in England this does not appear to be the case as much. He writes: "If we take a fairly broad historical cross-section of exemplary novels—from *Tom Jones* (1749) to *Great Expectations* (1861)—we are struck by the stability of narrative conventions and basic cultural assumptions" (Moretti 181). Additionally, he points out that England had already experienced revolution (between 1640 and 1688), that she was relatively unaffected by Napoleon and his troupes as well as the French Revolution of 1789 (Moretti 181). Although Moretti paints a picture of British literary stability and conformity during this period, he does not believe the appropriation of the *Bildungsroman* form of the novel in England to be without interest or dynamism.

A Sampling of English Versions of the Bildungsroman

Like Moretti, but 70 years earlier, Susanne Howe focused on the British inheritance of the German *Bildungsroman* form. She admits that tracing the direct influence of the publication of *Wilhelm Meister* on the development of the British *Bildungsroman* is quite difficult. She writes: "The line at which the direct effect of *Wilhelm Meister* ceases, and independent English variations on the theme begin, is blurred and uncertain. Two languages and literary traditions, and two national cultures during a complicated period of their history, have helped make it so" (Howe 7). What she and others like Moretti are perhaps more concerned with are the larger literary or non-literary views of self-development and enlightenment that crossed national boundaries during a period when the novel as a genre was still young and often under appreciated. Howe continues by identifying what she perceives to be other equally important aspects that shaped the British apprenticeship novel. She names Rousseau and Byron's confessional literature as well as *Werther*, with its "world-weariness" and character introspection, as influential in England's version of the genre (Howe 7-8). But perhaps the greatest idea that filtered through and was taken up by writers of the British *Bildungsroman* is Thomas Carlyle's conception of the "Gospel of Work" (Howe 10). Carlyle's 1824 translation of *Wilhem Meister* highlighted, perhaps more than the original, the necessity of work in completing apprenticeships for a trade for life in general. Howe believes that "[through] Carlyle the sane and corrective power of action was the moral lesson that *Wilhelm Meister* taught its English readers and imitators, and Goethe's eighteenth-century *Bildung*, or harmonious self-development motif, became subsidiary" (10). Thus, the idea that anything worth having requires much work took precedence over related themes.

In his chapter entitled *The Conspiracy of the Innocents*, Moretti discusses in detail the peculiarities of the British *Bildungsroman*. He begins with the notion of youth, which undoubtedly figures prominently in European *Bildungsromane*, but reveals that youthful ideologies generally have a longer lasting power, both good and bad, over mature characters in British novels. He cites *Tom Jones* as an example:

> The young hero's [Tom's] numerous erotic exploits are the very opposite of what we call 'experiences'. They are mere digressions . . . and they will never shed a different light on, nor force Tom from, the straight and narrow path of asexual love, of *childhood* love. Contrary to *Wilhelm Meister*, in the English novel the most significant experiences are not those that alter but those which confirm the choices made by childhood 'innocence.' (Moretti 182)

Yet Moretti also makes it clear that a certain "devaluation of youth" occurs because the more a character relies on the special insights of his youth, the less happiness and development he will find in adulthood (Moretti 184). In addition, English society, because of its structure and stability, creates just the "right space" for its youth. "Channeled into places and activities tightly secluded from the rest of the world (boarding schools, sport), English youth could not possibly identify with those symbolic values—indefiniteness, social and spiritual mobility, 'giddiness of freedom'—which were its essence on the Continent" (Moretti 184-85). Therefore, youth, understood in many novels as an advantage because a young character has his age, independence, relative liberty, and possibility all working in his favor, becomes devalued in this British conceptualization. In contrast to continental *Bildungsromane*, Moretti also suggests that many British *Bildungsromane* are merely fairy tales featuring the paradigm of good versus evil. He cites for instance, *Waverley, David Copperfield*, and *Great Expectations* (Moretti 185). "[The] hero [is] at the mercy of those who think little of him and his abilities, who mistreat him and even threaten his life" (qtd in Moretti 186). Furthermore, often the protagonist is a common and innocent "anybody" [Tom (Jones) and Jane (Eyre)] who faces evil which comes from above or below, never from the same social strata as the protagonist (Moretti 189, 200). Finally, Moretti notes that protagonists of British *Bildungsromane*, not unlike Wilhelm, Lucien, and Frédéric, do leave their homes, but their journeys are forced and not taken on their own volition. "The journey, and the mobility that goes with it, cannot therefore be seen by them as the ideal opportunity to try out new identities. It is just the opposite, a long and bewildering detour in which the roles they play in the course of time are merely disguises—unnatural, and sometimes repugnant—dictated by necessity" (Moretti 203). Nevertheless, these are accounts of youth and this period's life experiences, whether good or bad, will enlighten or confirm either positively or negatively the development of the individual.

The Bildungsroman in the Late-Nineteenth Century

While the novel in general and the *Bildungsroman,* because of its association as a sub-genre, had long been considered the ugly and unappreciated stepchild of modern literature, critics nonetheless continued their processes of defining the novel well into the late-nineteenth century. In his *Aesthetik oder Wissenschaft des Schönen* of 1857, Friedrich Theodor Vischer viewed the novel in a similar light as Hegel. In other words, the novel was the modern form of the epic and the novelist's purpose was to "rescue scraps of poetry—what Vischer terms 'grüne Stellen' [green spaces]—from an increasingly prosaic world" (Kontje 25). He believes the best way to accomplish this is to focus the novel on the individual unit of the family and on individual and interior self-development

(Kontje 25). Accordingly, Arthur Schopenhauer believes that the best novels are those which focus on the family to the exclusion of the technological advances and innovations of the rest of the world (Kontje 25). Numerous publications appeared championing the family. In 1853 in fact, the first issue of *The Garden Bower*, a literary journal for the public at large, featured a picture of a family sitting together around an older family member and protected by the arbor of lush greenery (Kontje 26). Four years later, Adalbert Stifter features the family in *Der Nachsommer* [*Indian Summer*], an Austrian *Bildungsroman* which carries the message that "'[the] family is what our times need,' much more than art, science, progress, or all those other things that seem so desirable" (Kontje 26). In addition, focus on the family unit in the novel brought about a "reassertion of the masculinity of the Bildungsroman" (Kontje 27). Certainly, female characters did abound in *Bildungsromane*, but they were there to insure that the male characters developed appropriately. According to Vischer, "the woman functions as a poetic oasis in the desert of modernity" (Kontje 27).

Wilhelm Dilthey, the critic, mistakenly we now know thanks to Fritz Martini, long thought to have coined the term B*ildungsroman*, contributed nonetheless to the ongoing discussion of the novel of development. Two late-nineteenth century publications are particularly noteworthy. In 1887, *The Poetic Imagination* chronicled Dilthey's yearning for a national German writer to pen the national novel. Although much political and literary unification had taken place especially since the early 1870s, Dilthey still felt an "absence of national consciousness, of the . . . impertinence of German Classicism as a guiding aesthetic in an age of aesthetic upheaval, of productivity that has lost all familiar bearing" (Corngold 76). Even though Dilthey continued to find inspiration in traditional literary Classicism, he also felt that aesthetic and poetic principles of the early-nineteenth century no longer applied to the realities of the late-nineteenth century. Dilthey writes: "Our [German] poetics . . . is still alive here and there on the lecturer's rostrum but no longer in the consciousness of the leading artists or critics, and only there would it be [truly] alive. . . . It [is] all over for the principles of that poetics which once upon a time in idyllic Weimar had been debated by Schiller, Goethe, and Humboldt" (qtd. in Corngold 77). In 1906, Dilthey, in his *Das Erlebnis und die Dichtung* [*Experience and Poetry*], presents his most oft referenced definition of *Bildungsroman*. He writes:

> Beginning with Wilhelm Meister and Hesperus, they [*Bildungsromane*] all depict the youth of that time, how he enters life in a blissful daze, searches for kindred souls, encounters friendship and love, but then how he comes into conflict with the hard realities of the world and thus matures in the course of manifold life-experiences, finds himself, and becomes certain of his task in the world. (qtd. in Kontje 29)

While this sounds a bit too perfect with its harmonious interactions and happy ending à la Christian Gottfried Körner[9], and even though it is true that Dilthey was taken to task by critics like Bernd Peschken and others, Dilthey's proclamation, when examined more closely, reveals an alternate means of interpretation. For example, Kontje notes the Dilthey admits that Goethe purposefully crafted his work so as to eliminate conflict and difficulty and accentuate harmony and unity. He also reminds us that Dilthey is certain to situate Goethe's masterpiece in the proper historical context—"the era of the Bildungsroman [was] an age long past that the current reader can read about with nostalgia" (29). Being reminded of these two viewpoints, Dilthey's definition now no longer offers such a simplistic perspective of *Wilhelm Meister* or the initial *Bildungsromane* in general. All in all, this definition will influence often reactionary critical thought concerning the *Bildungsroman* for decades to come. Finally, one last Dilthey legacy demonstrates the breadth of influence generated by his work on the genre. Dilthey insists that the *Bildungsroman* be separated theoretically from the common autobiography. Acknowledging similarities between the two, Dilthey nevertheless "observes that this type of novel, unlike the self-biography, 'consciously and artistically presents the universal human in a life's course.'... The apprenticeship novel [*Bildungsroman*] as a whole, he concludes, presents the path toward personality as the final form of human existence" (Shaffner 13). It is certain that Dilthey played a great role in theorizing the *Bildungsroman*; however, many other critics contributed as well.

Literary Critics Continue the Tradition

> The Bildungsroman chronicles *"the protagonist's mental, spiritual, and emotional development..."* and is a *"novel that describes the psychic development of an individual from the beginning up to the attainment of a definite life-form"* Christine Touaillon's definition in *Reallexikon der deutschen Literaturgeschichte*, 1925

The late-nineteenth and early-twentieth centuries brought several differing points of view with regards to the *Bildungsroman*. A 1904 article by Heinrich Driesmans suggests that the *Bildungsroman*, or as he calls it the *Erziehungsroman* or Educational Novel, continues well into the nineteenth century (Kontje 30). This sits in direct opposition to Dilthey's notions of the *Bildungsroman* which he situates within nostalgia of the historical past. "In the course of the nineteenth century Driesmans notes a gradual change,...a sort of Darwinian interest in questions of heredity, race, and breeding. Novelists no longer portray healthy, typical figures but concentrate on the psychopathology of the abnormal individual who is viewed as the product of 'a hereditary deterioration and physiological impoverishment' (qtd. in Kontje 30-1). Kontje notes the importance of Driesmans's essay lies in the fact that it declares the nineteenth century novel first, as the continuation of a style of writing begun in the eighteenth century and not something entirely new and second, as "the German novel moving in the direction of the European naturalist novel" (31). This second perspective was understood in a negative light. In 1906, a more positive analysis entitled "The More Recent German Bildungsroman" appears. In his text, Herman Anders Krüger expresses his nationalistic view that Germany is her own *Bildungsroman* hero (Kontje 31). As the genre developed so too had Germany herself— "Krüger identifies the year of German unification as an important stage in the development of the national character: German military prowess provides external confirmation of the spiritual maturation of the German people" (Kontje 31). In ways similar to those of Krüger, Thomas Mann sees the connection between the developing *Bildungsroman* and developing Germany. In a newspaper article from 1916, Mann declares the *Bildungsroman* to be "typically German, legitimately national;" yet, "he views the development of the German novel in the later nineteenth century as a process of moving away from this national genre toward the adoption of some highly un-German tendencies: politicization, literarization, intellectualization, radicalization . . . which causes the decline of the Bildungsroman" (Kontje 35). Over time, Mann's perceptions of the *Bildungsroman* changed and he began to accept more radical and revolutionary ideologies and behaviors. In Kontje's words: "The 'unpolitical man' [Mann] who just a few years earlier had railed against the corruption of a truly German genre of personal cultivation now hails Goethe as the author of an increasingly public, democratic, even political novel" (36). Additionally, W. Witte, a late-twentieth century critic, argues that Mann is "the novelist best suited to bridge that gap between the German and European novel tradition" (Kontje 71). In 1924, Mann published *Der Zuaberberg* [*The Magic Mountain*] wherein he presents his own changing political ideas through the self-development of the protagonist Hans Castorp. Finally, by 1925 the term *Bildungsroman* officially appeared in a dictionary of literary terms. Christine Touaillon's entry in the *Reallexikon der deutschen Literaturgeschichte* stressed "the protagonist's mental, spiritual, and emotional development, she identifies the apprenticeship novel as a 'novel that describes the psychic development of an individual from the beginning up to the attainment of a definite life-form'" (Shaffner 12). She also endeavors to delineate differences between the novel of education [*Erziehungsroman*] and the apprenticeship novel [*Bildungsroman*], two distinct sub-genres of the novel that have over the years inattentively conflated.

Many critics accepted and promoted the idea of parallel progression of the *Bildungsroman* as a genre with Germany's growth as a nation, but not until the twentieth century did the *Bildungsroman* appear connected to the promotion of fascist and Nazi ideologies. In the years preceding World War II, one such novel, *Volk ohne Raum* [*Nation Without Room*], written by Hans Grimm, recounts the story of protagonist Cornelius Friebott who sets off to Africa on a mission to expand Germany and her influence there. In 1937, critic Edgar Kirsch notes that Friebott was "[at] first uncertain of his role in the world, [but he] progresses toward an understanding of his calling—to affirm Germany over every-thing" (Kontje 41). New interpretations of the *Bildungsroman* lead to a move-ment from focus on the development and maturation of the individual to that of a society. Kontje also mentions the 1939 Charlotte Kehr dissertation that "traces a straightforward progression of the German novel away from a dangerously exaggerated individualism toward an ostensibly genuine 'völkisch-nationale Tradition' that places the energy of the individual in the service of the *Volk*" and thus offers a more radical proclamation and reclamation of German culture and identity (41-2).

World War II brought social, political, physical, and psychological destruc-tion to Germany. During the two decades following the war, the literary elite felt that perhaps the best way to recover what was left of Germany's cultural great-ness was to return, without deference to politics, to the classics, those warm and comfortable literary texts of the late-eighteenth and nineteenth centuries (Kontje 47). Numerous post-war critics weighed in with varying literary perspectives. Already mentioned above are Fritz Martini and T. J. Reed; however others, in-cluding Hans Heinrich Borcherdt, Karl Schlechta, and Werner Hoffman, con-tributed to ongoing discussions concerning the genre.

Borcherdt, who had in 1941 promoted Nazi ideologies using material from Grimm's *Nation Without Room*, now based his theories of collective develop-ment on Goethe's much older Wilhelm Meisters Wanderjahre (Kontje 45). Kontje adds, "The link between Germanness and the Bildungsroman also re-mains intact as the classical texts not only provide answers to the questions of the current age but also eternal solutions to the quest for the German form of life" (45). Borcherdt's ideas have not really changed, warns Kontje; more than likely, this is simply a "slight shift in rhetoric" (46).

While Borcherdt seems to be doing the same old thing just in a different way, Schlechta does present something new. Flying in the face of numerous critics over decades of analysis, Schlechta posits that Wilhelm does not success-fully fulfill his *Bildung* in the *Lehrjahre* or the *Wanderjahre*. In fact, cites Kontje, "the *Wanderjahre* becomes the negative fulfillment of the *Lehrjahre*, a social dystopia rather than the democracy envisioned by the older Thomas Mann" (46). Schlechta's harsh criticism of the guiding Tower Society from the novel was viewed for many years simply as his attack on the German govern-ment that brought the downfall of the nation years before. According to Kontje "[it] is important to note however, that although Schlechta spares no scorn for the Tower Society, he never criticizes Goethe. Instead, he reads the text with meticulous care to reveal how its surface humanism and concern for *Bildung* conceals another, often frighteningly brutal world of totalitarian control" (47). Schlechta's analyses were ignored for years because they appeared so radical and off the mark; yet in the years to follow, his evaluations became more and more accepted by the scholarly community (Kontje 48).

For his part, Hoffmann, writing in the late 1960s, fought against stringent qualifying factors for inclusion in the category of the *Bildungsroman*, an argu-ment he shared with François Jost author of the 1969 article "La Tradition du

'Bildungsroman'." Hoffmann claims that certain novels such as Grimmel-shausen's *Simplicissimus* of 1669 could be termed a *Bildungsroman*, even though it was published before Goethe's famed late-eighteenth century *Lehrjahre* and features alternate means to self-development and an overall rejection of the world in its conclusion (Kontje 50). He believes that to be classified as a novel of development, not all of the traditionally accepted *Bildungsroman* characteristics need be present. Hoffman's and Jost's evaluations and pronouncements are important because they lead to a wider application of the term *Bildungsroman*. Jost's article investigates French and other European national literatures in terms of being novels of development and enables critics to begin considering novels with female protagonists or novels by and about non-westerners as *Bildungsromane*.

Feminists Critics Take Up the Bilidungsroman

> *"Yet the novels written by women writers in recent years suggest that the Bildungsroman may well be acquiring a new function as an articulation of women's new sense of identity and increasing movement into public life"*
> Rita Felski, "The Novel of Self-Discovery: A Necessary Fiction?"

As critics focus their analyses of the *Bildungsroman* through the lens of the latest twentieth century literary theories [Poststructuralism, Psychoanalysis and Post-Colonialism]; in the late 1970s and '80s, a new group of scholars begins to examine the novel of development from feminist perspectives. In 1982, Jeanine Blackwell, flying in the face of long held assumptions, proclaims that protagonists in *Bildungsromane* could indeed be female. Her study, *"Bildungsroman mit Dame,"* cites two early novels, Sophie von LaRoche's *Geschichte des Fräulein von Sternheim* (1771) and Friederike Helene Unger's *Julchen Grünthal* (1784) that exhibit female protagonists who develop to a certain degree throughout the course of the novel (Kontje 105). Ultimately, what Blackwell reveals, even in later novels, is quite a negative outcome. Women characters, like their real life sisters of the nineteenth century, fare badly. Novels of this period "examine the mechanics of masochism, resignation, and voluntary celibacy as they shape personal development" (178-79). Similarly, Elizabeth Abel, Marianne Hirsch, and Elizabeth Langland present perspectives of female sacrifice and alienation in the process of becoming and developing. Their collection of essays, *The Voyage In: Fictions of Female Development*, treats texts which demonstrate the difficulties and dead ends of the *Bildungsprozess* for a female *Bildungsheld*. Perhaps these lines from their introduction best summarize the intention of their volume:

> A distinctive female "I" implies a distinctive values system and unorthodox developmental goals, defined in terms of community and em-

pathy rather than achievement and autonomy. The fully realized and individuated self who caps the journey of the Bildungsroman may not represent the development goals of women, or of women characters. Female fictions of development reflect the tensions between the assumptions of a genre that embodies male norms and the values of its female protagonists. The heroine's developmental course is more conflicted, less direct: separation tugs against the longing for fusion and the heroine encounters the conviction that identity resides in intimate relationships, especially those of early childhood. The deaths in which these fictions so often culminate represent less developmental failures than refusal to accept an adulthood that denies profound convictions and desires. (10-11)

Susan J. Rosowski's chapter in this volume entitled, "The Novel of Awakening," discusses the different form novels of development can take when a female figures as protagonist. Rosowski's text is one of the first to probe the variances between the male *Bildungsroman* and its female counterpart. Rosowski suggests that some female *Bildungsromane* should in fact be termed novels of awakening because the female protagonist "awakens" to the realization that her inward development puts her at a distance from the nature of the rest of the world. According to Rosowski, "The protagonist's growth results typically not with 'an art of living,' as for her male counterpart, but instead with a realization that for a woman such an art of living is difficult or impossible: it is an awakening to limitations" (49). Sadly, many feminist critics do not find much that is uplifting or empowering in female novels of development.

In 1986, Esther K. Labovitz suggested that "[f]or the eighteenth and nineteenth century German fictional heroine, as for the real life figures, the concept of *Bildung* virtually passed her by" (qtd. in Kontje 108). Labovitz contends that the female *Bildungsroman* did not appear until the twentieth century and then it served to revive what was believed to be a passé genre by infusing it with a vitality lacking in the novels by and about males. She proposes that the male *Bildungsroman* has disappeared fault of a "pluralistic and fragmented society" and that its rightful successor, the female *Bildungsroman*, although late to arrive on the scene, invites discussion concerning its promising future (Labovitz 8). Theorist Rita Felski classifies female *Bildungsromane* into two categories. First, there is the "feminine appropriation of the [traditional] Bildungsroman" which is simply the story of a "female protagonist [who] follows a path similar to that of the nineteenth-century male protagonist of the Bildungsroman" (qtd. in Kontje 108). Felski adds that the female *Bildungsroman* while similar in numerous ways to the traditional *Bildungsroman*, distinguishes itself from its predecessor in that instead of full integration into society, women characters gain self-reliance or acceptance into "'the feminist group, the communal household'" (Kontje 108). Second, the "novels of awakening" constitute the alternate form of female Bildungsroman. This type "traces a process of self-recognition rather than one of development" (qtd. in Kontje 109). Felski remains optimistic about the developments in the female Bildungsroman and its future despite criticism from others that she softpedals innovative work in areas of female expression such as Cixous's *l'écriture féminine*. "The Bildungsroman can assume," according to Felski, "'a new function as an articulation of women's new sense of identity and increasing movement into public life'" (qtd in Kontje 109).

Yet another critic who presents even more positive perspectives on female novels of development is Lorna Ellis. Ellis maintains that male *Bildungsromane* and female *Bildungsromane* are not as different as most feminist critics insist. She calls them two versions of the same genre and takes on Annis Pratt, Susan Fraiman [*Unbecoming Women*], and Able, Hirsch, and Langland in order to demonstrate that what Pratt has termed "growing down"[10] is all about perspective and that "growing down paradoxically enables growing up" (Ellis 18). These two forms of growth are part of the same process, and deciding whether to call the protagonist's growth 'up' or 'down' is similar to deciding whether to call a glass half full or half empty, both descriptions are accurate, but neither tells the whole story" (Ellis 18). Naturally, Ellis concedes several points. For example, she admits that many female protagonists never acquire the means or are able to create for themselves opportunities for continued development. But she is quick to point out that even male protagonists often find themselves in similar positions. Ellis notes:

> Just as Emma Woodhouse gives up her hobby of matchmaking and molds her will to Knightley's expectations, so too does Wilhelm Meister give up his adolescent dream of a theatrical career and conform his expectations and desires to those of his future wife and her brother. Just as Jane Eyre's adult life as the constant companion of Rochester lacks the adventure of her penniless days as a student, teacher and governess, so too does David Copperfield's adult life with Agnes forego the adventures that were inherent in his contacts with the Macawber and Peggoty families. . . . In both [male and female *Bildungsromane*], maturation comes at the expense of adventure and some personal autonomy. (19)

It is conceivable that for some these examples might not be enough to prove Ellis's assertion that in essence the male and female *Bildungsromane* are not as different as critics have made them out to be. To further what this author believes to be an already solid point, she identifies and discusses a novel of development with a female protagonist published prior to Goethe's *Wilhelm Meister*.

Like Blackwell, Ellis disagrees with Labovitz's claim that the female *Bildungsroman* did not exist until the twentieth century. Madame de Graffigny's *Lettre d'une peruvienne* (1747), which chronicles the personal development of Zilia, a Peruvian woman living in France, not only appeared in the eighteenth century, but it predates Goethe's *Wilhelm Meister* by 48 years. Ellis also categorizes Eliza Haywood's *The History of Miss Betsy Thoughtless* (1751) as a female *Bildungsroman*. She contends that many events and incidents in *Betsy Thoughtless* are quite similar to those in the average *Bildungsroman*. Yet she acknowledges further that differences between the two varieties of the genre, such as the kind of alienation felt by female versus male protagonists, serve to "[create] a model for female development that provided women with a sophisticated understanding of their constricted place in society while encouraging them to manipulate societal expectation in order to promote their own welfare" (23). Working within the system, within the limits of gendered cultural and societal inequality, is one solution Ellis sees for female protagonists of the *Bildungsroman*. Still, there are those who claim rightly that this forces women to have to play patriarchy's game. Even Ellis recognizes this problematic situation:

> By teaching their protagonists how to understand and work within the limits of their societies, authors of female Bildungsromane allow their heroines to mature or 'grow up'—to understand themselves and their relationship to their environment in order to maintain some form of agency. However, the process of learning to understand and work within the limits of society simultaneously forces the heroine to decrease her sphere of action or to "grow down." She must give up those aspects of her independence that separate her from patriarchal society, and she must find ways to reconcile her view of herself with others' expectations of her. (18)

This qualified power is better than no power and learning to "work within the system" is after all learning and developing toward selfhood. Ellis cites Elizabeth Bennet's [*Pride and Prejudice*] learned "humility" in order to gain the "social and economic advantage of becoming mistress of Pemberley" and this while maintaining her autonomous abilities "to think and judge separately" (18). Whether one chooses to side with critics such as Blackwell, Abel, Hirsch, and Langland who see limitation, inadequacy, and too much compromise in female *Bildungsromane* when compared to male versions, or with Ellis and others who, while conceding certain persistent inequalities and difficulties, nonetheless see most novels of female development as positive, ground-gaining narratives; one must admit that as the times change, the possibilities for balanced female *Bildungsromane*, novels that reflect more genuine processes of development for female protagonists, increase dramatically.

So far the essence and history of the traditional *Bildungsroman* have been established and attempts have been made to suggest the various movements, forces and ideologies that early on influenced this genre. In addition, the presentation of a survey of the various differing characteristics of the *Bildungsroman* as it appeared in its German, French, and English varieties reminds one not only of the growing influence of the novel during the nineteenth century, but also of the contributions to this genre made by the Germans. However, the focus of this study concerns African literature and it is to that twentieth-century phenomenon that our direction now turns.

The Possibilities and Future of a Genre: The African Bildungsroman

Not since the days of the Weimar Classicists has the *Bildungsroman* belonged solely to late eighteenth century Germany. Even as the genre reached its fulfillment in Goethe's *Wilhelm Meisters Lehrjahre*, the work most critics recognize as the prototypical novel of individual development and formation, the parallel spirits of individuality and reason swiftly swept the European continent. French, English, German and Russian authors offered their versions of the process of individuation during the nineteenth century. Yet during these many years, Goethe's exemplar text and Dilthey's definition—"a regulated development within the life of the individual is observed, each of its stages has its own intrinsic value and is at the same time the basis for a higher stage. The dissonances and conflicts of life appear as the necessary growth points through which the individual must pass on his way to maturity and harmony," (Abel, Hirsch, and Langland 5-6)—entrenched rather strict and idealistic notions, especially those relating to the hero's interaction with his social surroundings and sexual activity, regarding novels treating individual development. In fact, not only do the earliest *Bildungsromane* "presuppose a range of social options available only to men," but they revealed the near impossibility of a true and authentic *Bildungsprozess* for anyone—Wilhelm or flesh and blood humans (Abel, Hirsch, and Langland 7). Rigorous adherence to an idealistic definition of the *Bildungsroman* soon leads scholars to a literary dead end, recall Jeffrey L. Sammons's theory of the "missing *Bildungsroman*;" yet what the Germans were up to in the late eighteenth century can certainly inform scholarly work on individuation in the twentieth and twenty first centuries.

Many critics, including Hoffman, Jost, Blackwell, Howe, Abel, Hirsch, Langland, Kontje, Rosowski, Labovitz, Felski, LeSeur, and Stratto agree that expansions in understanding and application can be granted to the sub-genre to allow for an updated appreciation of it within modern and contemporary mileux. The catalogue of critics cited above each proffers his or her own theoretical contributions thus laying the foundation for continued study of the modern *Bildungsroman*. Hoffman and Jost claim that every single attribute of the original *Bildungsroman* need not be present for a text to be classified as a type of *Bildungsroman*. Howe, in her quotation that opens this chapter, paints an optimistic picture of the future for the sub-genre, predicting new forms and infinite possibility. Kontje, in the conclusion of his survey of the sub-genre, concurs with Howe's prognosis. Abel, Hirsch, Langland, and Labovitz, each in her own way, open the way for investigation of female protagonists in novels of development, while Rosowski and Felski examine the novel of awakening, a variant of the female *Bildungsroman*. Finally, LeSeur and Stratton, as well as Androne and Veit-Wild extend *Bildung* interpretations to novels written by and about

Antilleans, African-Americans, and Africans. Nonetheless, questions of narrative language and use of predominantly Western literary theories continue to render various analyses of African literature quite complex.

In the 1970s and 80s, the *bolekaja* critics (Chinweizu, Onwuchekwa Jemie, and Ihechukwu Madubuike) felt certain authors such as Wole Soyinka, John Pepper Clark, and Christopher Okigbo over-appropriated English language attributes and other characteristics in their writing resulting in a written product described as "old-fashioned, craggy, unmusical [in terms of] language, obscure, and in accessible [in terms of] diction" (Ashcroft, Griffiths, and Tiffin, *The Empire Writes Back* 128). On the contrary, the group felt that texts written by authors such as Chinua Achebe exhibited simple, accessible language which remained connected to oral components of African culture and retained African rhythms and textures (Ashcroft, Griffiths, and Tiffin, *The Empire Writes Back* 128). Classification of texts as African, English/english[11] or French certainly remains contentious; however the stance taken here in this study has been one which aligns more or less with Achebe's view. That is to say, when African writers use English or French, the Western language "is made to bear the weight and the texture of a different experience. In so doing it [English or French] becomes a different language" (Ashcroft, Griffiths, and Tiffin, *The Post-Colonial Studies Reader* 284). Thus a novel authored by an African is an African novel and the narrative language, permeated with elements often deemed "foreign" or "non-standard" from a Western perspective, serves to confirm this. The novel's "nationality" is not necessarily dependent upon the language used in the narrative but on the nationality of its author and the culture and tradition conveyed by the author's content and word choice. Likewise, the location of the author's residence, be it London or Paris, New York or Toronto, does not determine a work's "nationality."

Despite the fact that critics have applied *Bildung* theories to non-Western works, superimposing the concepts regarding and theories surrounding such an obviously Western literary genre as those relating to the *Bildungsroman* onto African texts written in English and French might generate debate at best and application difficulties at worst. Perhaps the most memorable and witty rejection of theories intended to be used in analyses of texts originating throughout the African Diaspora is Soyinka's denunciation of the tenets of Senghor, Césaire and Diop's *Négritude* movement developed primarily for use with poetry in the first half of the twentieth century. Soyinka's famous remark, "a tiger does not proclaim its tigritude," unmistakably declared his view that literary texts from the Diaspora should never be subject to the theoretical "categories and features of the colonizing culture" (Ashcroft, Griffiths, and Tiffin, *The Empire Writes Back* 128). While he believed African (or Caribbean or African-American) texts stand on their own merits, he later conceded the usefulness of such organizing paradigms as those detailed by the *Négritudists*. It is crucial however that referenced Western concepts harmonize with African texts under analysis without re-colonizing the intentions of the author or skewing her message.

Without a doubt, creative expression has existed in Africa for thousands of years. Traditional oral literature formed the foundation for later, contemporary developments in literature. Written texts existed certainly, as Owomoyela notes, but early on most African (and European for that matter) societies were composed of cultures of orality[12] and more importantly, the transmission of this oral art fed a culture that thrived on communal sharing of stories and tales "whose purposes [were] religious, entertaining, panegyrical, fictional, historical, medical, and so on" (1). Oral texts, sometimes referred to as "Orature," comprise epics, myths, legends, tales, poetry, dirges, and praise chants. Some of these are communicated by professional performers (referred to as *akéwì* in Yoruba, *maroki* in Hausa, *imbongi* in Zulu, *Djeli* in Mandinka, and *griot* in French) who are accompanied at times by musicians and troupes of secondary performers (Owomoyela 14). The repertoire of stories, songs, and chants becomes a living entity as it is expanded year after year. Because the community and its people's experiences over many years create the storehouse of material to be related given a certain circumstance, individual or original material was at times frowned upon. The characters in the stories are general in nature (many employ stock characters); they exist to communicate a broad idea without conferring too much attention on an individual (Owomoyela 21). In general, explains Owomoyela, "African societies do not deny the existence of individuals or of individual traits, but require that these be subjugated to the best interests of the group" (21). In contrast to oral literature, written African literature, especially the later publications, appears in general to feature differentiated individuals.

In the late 1930s and '40s, Senegalese students, who had scholarships to study in Paris, Leopold Sédar Senghor and Birago Diop, along with their Martiniquan collaborator Aimé Césaire and others worked to develop a general theory of Negro peoples of the Diaspora called *Négritude*. Mostly associated with poetry, the theory proclaimed civilization and validity of African cultures worldwide. One of the movement's first publications, *Anthologie de la nouvelle poésie nègre et malgache de langue française*, pressed for an understanding that African cultures across the Diaspora possessed unique and legitimate artistic standards and that well-established African poetry was not simply a weaker version of European verse. The anthology, prefaced and lauded by Jean-Paul Sartre, was only the first of several publications to appear. *Présence Africaine*, established by Alioune Diop in 1947 in Paris, proved also to be an important means for the dissemination of African literary criticism and theories. Beginning in 1957, *Présence Africaine* was published in both French and English allowing for a more widespread circulation of ideas and theories. These publications radiated in waves the positive message that all peoples of African descent (Africans, West Indians, African-Americans) should celebrate their dignity, distinctiveness, and unique aesthetic abilities.

The advent of the African novel coincided with several social, cultural, and historical factors. One of the first francophone African novels, *Les trois volontés de Malik* by Ahmadou Mapate Diagne, was published in 1930. Six years later,

Force-Bonté by Bakary Diallo appeared. Described as a "naïve panegyric of French civilization," Diallo's novel remained the most important publication in Africa for nearly a decade (Brench 4-5). Novels by the earlier writers tended to relate positive experiences concerning colonization and to demonstrate gratitude toward European nations for the "improvements" made in Africa. Furthermore, African novels benefited from a keen Western interest, brought about partly by the Modernist movement, in all things exotic, in short, all things African. In fact, the "flawed" English and simple linear plot of writers like Amos Tutuola were considered charming aspects of this new kind of literature and European publishers and editors, although they did "clean it up" a bit, dared not tamper too much with such "native" style. Owomoyela notes that "[what] the publishers and European readers valued (and continue to value) in Tutuola is his naïveté—he is the unspoiled African, a literary noble savage" (74). Inappropriate, but all too common, primitivist othering notwithstanding, the earlier African novels were popular in the West because readers were intrigued by their rather simplistic views of exotic cultures and their lenient references to colonialism; in short, these novels were something different—a novelty.

In the 1950s, novels came with more regularity. While images of society and the individuals' relationship to it never entirely faded away, African prose narratives from the mid-twentieth century on began to highlight, among other things, the individual paths and destinies of singular Africans. Chinua Achebe's *Things Fall Apart* followed Amos Tutuola's *The Palm-Wine Drinkard* of 1953 in 1958. A second generation of writers began publishing as many African countries experienced politically charged instability. For many nations, colonialism seemed to be making its retreat. Sudan and Ghana were the first countries to gain their independence (1956 and 1957 respectively) and such liberation appeared likely within a couple of years for all colonized peoples. Thus it was within such an environment that writers shared their perspectives on colonialism. European colonizers had long insisted their purposes for being in Africa included helping a backward people out of the lawless, godless, and illiterate states they were in. Unlike the first African prose writers whose imitative works tended to praise colonizers while highlighting the great things they had done for Africa, this new group of writers sought to show that Africa indeed was not as backward and uncivilized as many Europeans believed and that in fact colonialism had done more to hurt the continent than it had to help it. Achebe notes, "I will be quite satisfied if my novels (especially the ones I set in the past) did no more than teach my readers that their past—with all its imperfections—was not one long night of savagery from which the first Europeans acting on God's behalf delivered them" (59). *Things Fall Apart* chronicles the misfortunes brought about by the inherent destabilizing effects of clashing cultures on a central protagonist, Okonkwo, and his community. "Achebe makes a serious attempt," notes G. D. Killam, "to capture the strains and tensions of the experiences of Ibo people under the impact of colonialism [He] is able to view objectively the forces which irresistibly and inevitably destroyed traditional Ibo social ties and with them the quality of Ibo life" (14). Similarly, Francophone novelist Camara Laye proclaims Africa's distinction and grandeur. According to Owomoyela:

> In both cases one hears echoes of the [Négritude] poets' efforts to re-discover and proclaim African culture, Achebe for the benefit of Af-ricans themselves and Laye for all and sundry . . . . Generally the writer presents an idyllic picture of traditional life and explains the various elements in the most favorable light. The advent of the Euro-pean into that setting is regarded as traumatic and disruptive . . . . Chinua Achebe, whose writings exude an aura of tragedy, shows the unfortunate effects of European actions on African life . . . the disso-lution of traditional moorings, leaving the individual groping uncer-tainly in a new dispensation he does not understand. (82)

Hoping to feature Africa as Achebe does, Camara Laye sought to show the beauty and culture of Africa in his works. "For Camara Laye . . . the culture is something strong, eternal, and self-sufficient, able to contain the European im-pact without losing its essence" (Owomoyela 82). Indeed, the influence of colo-nization is certainly felt in Laye's *L'Enfant noir* [*The Dark Child*]. His privileg-ing of African culture is crystallized by Carroll Yoder: "In *L'Enfant noir* the narrator relates his journey from home in terms of ever-expanding concentric circles that separate him from traditional life. But whereas colonial writers had considered the pilgrimage to Paris as an ascending path leading to human per-fection, Laye reverses the process with each of the child's steps leading him farther from original perfection" (111). Post-colonial writers sought to commu-nicate through fiction (often semi-autobiography) the degree to which the colo-nial project overturned traditional African societal mores, confused African val-ues, and redirected paths to individual and community progress and development.

With ever-expanding opportunities for publication, African writers, from the 1960s on, added quickly to the body of African literature. In the 1970s and '80s, women writers like Buchi Emecheta, Bessie Head, and Mariama Bâ began to make their presence widely known. While this was a boon for writing and for women in general, most critics are quick to point out that women's fiction actu-ally began almost a decade earlier. In 1966, Flora Nwapa and Grace Ogot pub-lished their first novels, *Efuru* and *The Promised Land* respectively. Needless to say, their invisibility was quite simply a product of societal bias, post-colonial anxiety, and the general favoring of representative male authors who in each case eclipsed the spotlight that could have shone on the female authors (Achebe over Nwapa in Nigeria and Ngũgĩ over Ogot in Kenya). Even though early on, women writers seemed "invisible,"[13] within a few years their fiction and the critical response to it flourished.

Analyses of African works as *Bildungsromane* provide great insight into complex issues represented in a body of fiction about individuals in the process of learning about themselves, about the world, and the interrelationship between the two. Although late-eighteenth century Germany is far away in time, place, and context from twentieth century Africa, there are similar personal discoveries and processes of development taking place on both sides of the Mediterranean Sea. The [semi-] autobiographical nature of certain early African novels and their concern with the qualified development of individual protagonists point to some common characteristics. In addition, colonialism traces its roots to the height of nineteenth-century European growth and expansion. The connection between the German genre and African novels of development lies ultimately in the fact that African colonial history is inextricably linked to European history.

Besides the five novels that structure the main analysis of this study, Achebe's *Things Fall Apart* and Ngũgĩ's *Weep Not, Child* as well as Laye's *L'Enfant Noir* and Mongo Beti's *Le pauvre Christ de Bomba* trace courses of individuation and self-formation not unlike those of the *Bildung* protagonists of the eighteenth and nineteenth centuries. Many post-colonial African texts contain explorations and examinations of the condition of colonized individuals. Such twentieth-century selves, undergoing necessary processes of re-discovery and re-definition, yield insightful information on the status of the modern *Bildungsroman*. More subtly, travel to areas away from familiar native soil to facilitate new experiences coupled with an internal drive to learn about the world while critical of it constitute still more similarities between German and African *Bildung* fiction.

In her study on African-American and West Indian Black writers, Geta Le-Seur points out that "during the 1950s the trend toward portraiture and individualization saw Blacks exploring their identities" (19). She notes in addition that many of these (autobiographical) novels chronicle the lives of children as they grow and learn more about the world around them. Speaking in generalities, LeSeur adds, "as the hero or heroine [of these novels] reaches maturity, each will typically feel bondage, the multiple constraints of living, often represented by the pressures of the cruel city. The creative vision, however, restores freedom, and the child's questioning sense of outward things is parent of the understanding child; the quickened imagination outlives the troubled 'season of youth'" (20). Obviously, black novels of development are ultimately different from their white counterparts because "of a different set of sociological and historical contexts. . . . With Emancipation, in the United States and the Caribbean, the newly independent nations, and the African nations' revolutions of the 1960s, a new kind of literature had to be written as an affirmation of those emancipations" (LeSeur 21). While most of LeSeur's remarks deal mainly with African-American and Black West Indian novels, certainly many of her comments might be applied to analyses of novels from across the African Diaspora.

One must be reminded, as discussed earlier, that modern day prospective *Bildungsromane* need not include all of the characteristics of the eighteenth and nineteenth-century European model. Thriving genres change and develop; they adapt to the times and issues in question. The changes the German *Bildungsroman* underwent as it crossed European national boundaries have already been discussed. It is but one conceivable step more from these well documented

French, Russian and English versions to an evaluation of African literature in terms of literature of development, of expansion, and of self-culture. In his conclusion, Kontje suggests that "[if] the Bildungsroman is the genre that portrays historical change, then recent studies of the genre show an interest in new ways of defining that change: in terms of the transformation of the public sphere; the restructuring of the family; and the codification of gender roles. Future studies may well…explore its applicability to non-Western cultures (111-12). Ten years earlier, Abel, Hirsch, and Langland wrote:

> It has become a tradition among critics of the *Bildungsroman* to expand the concept of the genre: first beyond the German prototypes, then beyond historical circumscription, now beyond the notion of Bildung as male and beyond the form of the developmental plot as linear, foregrounded narrative structure. [This] reformulation participates in a critical tradition by transforming a recognized historical and theoretical genre into a more flexible category whose validity lies in its usefulness as a conceptual tool. (13-4)

Feminist critics have for years been outraged over the paucity of critical insight on constructions of gender, what they preclude and what they enable, in novels of development. Thus the above adjustment in critical thinking and conception allows for broadened future investigations. This study undertakes not only a consideration of gender in the writings of late-twentieth century, female African novelists, but it also investigates the effects colonialism, independence and post-colonial society may have on the African female *Bildungsheld*.

In the spirit of Labovitz who believes in a bright future for female novels of development and Abel, Hirsch, and Langland who likewise see contemporary applications for a sub-genre steeped in conservative tradition and patriarchal resonance, this study undertakes an evaluation of late-twentieth century novels of development by African writers. Indeed critics such as Florence Stratton and Susan Andrade have already used the term *Bildungsroman* in reference to African fiction. But while their appellation certainly precedes this examination, this study intends to build upon that foundation they so boldly established and to offer further insights as to the concerns of Emecheta, Damgarembga, and Beyala when considered both separately and together. Outside this author's personal interest in the three chosen African writers of my corpus, they were selected because their texts depict the female *Bildung* heroine at a variety of life stages— from the innocence of a young child through the awakening of a young mother. Emecheta, Damgarembga, and Beyala represent three distinct African nations and thus varied cultures and traditions. While colonialism and its far-reaching effects in Africa and/or on the European continent rest at the heart of each of the five works, Emecheta, Dangarembga, and Beyala's publications cross sections of three decades [from 1972 to 1993] and examine periods of time from around 1934 to the present as defined by a given novel's date of publication. The novels therefore offer diachronic interpretations of that which is involved in individual development and formation expressed from the stance of three women writers who dare speak of possibility.

Notes

1 This was "...a short-lived but significant literary movement...which is generally regarded as marking the beginning if modern literary consciousness... [The participants] championed nature against culture, the individual against society, feeling against thought and spontaneity against trained response..." (Herd and Obermayer 262-63).

2 Much of the early criticism on the *Bildungsroman* perpetuated the clear sexism claimed by the genre. Similar to Howe's excerpt here, the earliest critics discussed development exclusively in male terms despite the fact that female novels of development existed before Goethe's prototypical *Wilhelm Meister* and that many female novels of development have been written since.

3 A religious movement in the Lutheran church in the seventeenth century emphasizing individual connections to God over organized, hierarchical and even orthodox religion.

4 *Goethes Wilhelm Meister und die Entwicklung des modernen Lebensideals.* Berlin, 1913.

5 For further discussion of the development of the reader of a novel see Dennis F. Mahoney's "The Apprenticeship of the Reader: The Bildungsroman in the 'Age of Goethe'" in James Hardin's *Reflection and Action: Essays on the Bildungsroman*, 1991.

6 This text was extensively revised and expanded and became *Wilhelm Meisters Lehrjahre*. The main action of *Theatralische Sendung* became but one incident in the *Lehrjahre* while the addition of several other points of intrigue rounds out the latter's new and improved storyline and character presentation.

7 For Balzac, for example, illusion is "not knowing the true value of things" (Moretti 167).

8 Paraphrase of Georg Simmel's "*Cultures omnia habentes , nihil possidentes*" from his essay "On the Concept of Tragedy in Culture" in *The Conflict in Modern Culture and Other Essays*, 1968.

9 Körner had earlier characterized *Wilhelm Meister* and other *Bildungsromane* in a letter to Schiller as having a "unity of the whole," "perfect equilibrium," and "harmony of freedom" (Kontje 10-1).

10 Pratt claims that in novels "'growing up female' has been in fact 'growing down,' 'a choice between auxiliary or secondary personhood, sacrificial victimization, madness, and death'" (Ellis 16).

11 For various perspectives concerning the use of English or French by African writers see Part IX entitled *Language* in Ashcroft, Griffiths and Tiffin's *The Post-Colonial Studies Reader*, 1995.

12 Christopher L. Miller prefers the term orality over illiteracy: "Illiteracy is a 'scriptocentric' term—it presupposes writing as the norm, and the absence of writing as a flaw. The shift in terminology from 'illiteracy' to 'orality' has important implications for the relations between the modern West and the third world" (68-9).

13 Florence Stratton reminds that the first novel in Heinemann's African Writers Series is by Achebe [*Things Fall Apart*] and the twenty-sixth, the first by a woman, is *Efuru* by Nwapa. Thirty male-authored texts later, Nwapa's *Idu* appears on the list (80).

Chapter 2

Having Eyes to See More: Emecheta's *Second-Class Citizen* as Modern Day *Bildungsroman*

> *"'Be as cunning as a serpent but as harmless as a dove,' [Adah]*
> *quoted to herself." Second-Class Citizen*

Nigerian novelist Buchi Emecheta's works are known for the manner in which complex issues of racial, gender, social, and economic inequalities in conjunction with the residual effects of British colonialism are treated. Arriving at an understanding of her texts requires an understanding of present day Nigeria's history. The four kingdoms and empires (The Northern Empire, The Calabar Kingdom, The Oduduwa Empire, and The Benin Empire) that make up present day Nigeria became occupied by British missionaries and explorers in the 1800s. On a mission to "save savage souls" as well as to harvest natural resources for European interests, the British organized the region in 1914 by combining the Northern and Southern Protectorates along with the colony of Lagos and called the new area Nigeria. In a short time, British occupation was established replete with a Governor-General. Nigeria did not see independence until October 1960. Because of colonization, the political dynamics, social phenomena, racial tensions and historical events of Nigeria are bound up in European history. Clearly, it is within this context, even though she writes in a postcolonial era, that Emecheta's works must be read and understood.

While other African women authors, most notably Ifeoma Okoye, Grace Ogot, Ama Ata Aidoo, and Flora Nwapa, wrote before Emecheta, their works generally ignite or invite less biting criticism concerning the above mentioned thematics. Nonetheless, Emecheta's writings both fall in line with and expand the issues of those writers who came before her. Accordingly, when Emecheta was questioned concerning her connection to other African female authors she responded by stating that she was "their new sister" (qtd. in Stratton 108). Susan Arndt has classified writing by African women authors into three categories: *reformist* literature, writing that critiques age old patriarchal structures without suggesting alternatives; *transformative* literature, writing that analyses men more directly while making the assumption that they can change for the better; and *radical* literature, writing that has given up all hope on men because they exhibit natural and immutable sexism and immorality.

Many, but certainly not all, of the authors who wrote before Emecheta, in other words the first wave of African women authors, have been placed in the *reformist* category. According to Arndt, texts that are *reformist* in nature critique

> *individual*, patriarchally-molded attitudes, norms and conventions, both century-old and modern, which discriminate against women and hinder their self-realization. Consequently, the criticism is only partial, and is usually brought forth in an undifferentiated way. Ultimately, it does not challenge the foundations of patriarchal society. *Reformist* African-feminist writers want to negotiate with the patriarchal society to gain new scope for women, but accept the fundamental patriarchal orientation of their society as a given fact. (82-3)

Arndt has grouped the writings of Grace Ogot, Ifeoma Okoye, and Flora Nwapa together in this initial category. Arndt continues her sorting by placing Emecheta in the dominant category in terms of quantity, the *transformative* feminist writers. These writers, in addition to Emecheta, include Mariama Bâ, Tsitsi Dangarembga, and Wanjira Muthoni. Their works consider "the ability of men—as a 'social group'—to transform. Moreover, the demands which are directed at men are more fundamental and extensive than those made in *reformist* literature (Arndt 84). Arndt's final category, *radical* feminist writers, includes writers who are generally born after most African countries became independent, that is to say after 1960, and their stance is that "men (as a social group) inevitably and in principle discriminate against, oppress and mistreat women. The men characters are 'by nature' or because of their socialization, hopelessly sexist and usually deeply immoral" (Arndt 85). Among other authors, Calixthe Beyala, the final author to be discussed in Chapters Five and Six, is classified as a *radical* feminist author. For this study, Arndt's categories provide an anchoring structure on which these writers' texts can be stretched out for diachronic study as they are examined in terms of the theory of the *Bildungsroman*.

A feminist Difference

"The assumption that the family is by definition patriarchal, the privileging of an individualistic worldview, and the advocacy of female separatism are often antithetical positions to many of the values and goals of black women and thus are hindrances to our association with feminism." Deborah K. King in "Multiple Jeopardy, Multiple Consciousness: The Context of Feminist Ideology"

Without a doubt, Emecheta is a feminist writer even while her novels, especially the two semi-autobiographical ones, *Second-Class Citizen* and *In the Ditch*, to be considered in this chapter and the next, are just as concerned with notions of equity and opportunity for all. Her stories relate the seemingly minor events of life; yet issues of personal growth and development, personal *Bildung*, greater than the sum of such incidents gain exposure and entreat consideration. At the 1986 Stockholm Conference for African Writers, Emecheta discusses her innate need to express herself through writing:

> I am just an ordinary writer, an ordinary writer who has to write, because if I didn't write I think I would have to be put in an asylum. Some people have to communicate, I happen to be one of them. I have tried several times to take university appointments and work as a critic, but each time I have packed up and left without giving notice. ("Feminism with a small 'f'!" 173)

Her compulsion to write has obliged her to chronicle that which is closest to and most central in her life. Most of her works resonate forcefully with the basic tenets of Western feminism, those that argue women's basic social and political equalities with men, and she has, on multiple occasions because of the themes in her works, been classified as a feminist.[1] Because of such a classification, Emecheta has felt the need to elucidate the aims of her project:

> For myself, I don't deal with great ideological issues. I write about the little happenings of everyday life. Being a woman, and African born, I see things through an African woman's eyes. I chronicle the little happenings in the lives of the African women I know. I did not know that by doing so I was going to be called a feminist. But if I am now a feminist then I am an African feminist with a small f. In my books I write about families because I still believe in families. I write about women who try very hard to hold their families together until it becomes absolutely impossible. ("Feminism with a small 'f'!" 175)

Emecheta acknowledges that her personal writing objectives do not align completely with those of Western feminist writers. While she generally recognizes contributions made by feminist writers and thinkers; instead of complete and vituperative male condemnations and exclusions or politically charged solutions, her works, largely due to her traditional African background, retain a focus on the family. In fact, the cohesion of the African family through even the worst of times takes priority. Her feminist perspectives focus on alternate areas of womens' lives as they reinscribe the objectives of the imperialistic qualities of white Western feminism.

While her works outwardly appear feminist in nature, they might be said simply to share some generalized concerns with Western feminism. This is the case because Emecheta is indeed concerned about the growth and development, in short, the burgeoning authentic selfhood, of her central protagonist Adah; yet Adah supports her husband until he becomes violent and loves and sacrifices for her five children. So many Western approaches to African literature serve only to reinforce stereotypes and in Cynthia Ward's terms "[reinscribe] the image of Africa as the dark continent where 'primitive' cultural practices must be guided into productive paths by enlightened Europeans" (qtd in Fishburn 20). Likewise, Chandra Mohanty asserts that Western feminist theories generally limit their scope and analysis solely to gender identities in dealing with women from developing cultures when a larger depiction to include class and ethnic identities is more comprehensive and appropriate (Mohanty 64). Hence, African writers of both sexes are especially wary of Western literary theory with its tendency to codify as "Other" or marginalize non-western people or ideologies or to treat "the production of the 'third world woman' as a singular monolithic subject" (Mohanty 52). African writers, like Emecheta and Ama Ata Aidoo believe that their works do not require any sort of Western filter of interpretation, even that of feminism. According to Aidoo, African women have always been fighters: "To try to remind ourselves and our brothers and lovers and husbands and colleagues that we also exist should not be taken as something foreign, as something bad. African women struggling both on behalf of themselves and . . . the wider community is very much a part of our heritage. We haven't learnt this from anybody abroad" (Emecheta, "Feminism with a small 'f'!" 183). Undeniably, Emecheta's works deal with gender issues; however, they are equally concerned with issues of race and class; all the more since the two semi-autobiographical works *Second-Class Citizen* and *In the Ditch* are principally set in London. While certain similarities of purpose between the works of African women and their Western sisters exist, the African works tend to deal with broader concepts—most notably the intersection of sexism, racism, and classism. Katherine Fishburn acknowledges summarily that

> African women do have much to complain about, and there is legitimate, impassioned political protest in their fiction. But this protest must be seen in a larger perspective than the one provided by (white Western) feminism or (white Western) socialism. Without this wider

perspective, it is just too easy to represent the lives of African women as so similar to ours that they can be judged on our terms. All too often this has meant, as Chandra Mohanty (1984) demonstrates, that Third World women's lives and cultures have been found to be inferior to ours. (22)

While Fishburn's judgement here is not the issue, the point that African literature is not legitimated through Western theory and critique is critical. African Literature exists and claims its own power and strength by its own merit. Yet, it is possible to formulate readings and evaluations of African literature through Western theory (feminist, *bildung*, etc) in so far as the theories are not presented as one-size-fits-all universals, and are dealt with honestly when incongruities become evident.

From Eighteenth Century Germany to Twentieth Century Africa

How is it possible to make a leap of application from German *Bildung* theory to African novels as *Bildungsromane*? As mentioned in Chapter One, this book is predicated on much work done by critics such as Hoffman, Jost, Blackwell, Hirsch, Abel, Langland, Rosowski, Labovitz, and Felski. From more flexible definitions of the sub-genre to the acknowledgement of women authors of female *Bildungsromane*, *Bildung* theory has proven useful for all novels portraying personal individuation regardless of place and time. The necessary evolution and current manifestation of the *Bildungsroman* now allow for broader and, it is believed, more revealing application.

Additionally, developing styles and aesthetics of African writers brought about change in theme, focus, and message in African novels. Most of the first well-known African writers [Tutuola, Diagne, Diallo, and Ogot] do not present in their novels overt, scathing protests of colonialism and its consequences on their home soil. Among other things, alleged simplified use of the English language, use of native proverbs, and perceived difficulty with verbal expression characterize these early texts. As more opportunities for writers and writing came about, African texts began to deal with the various realities of life during and after colonial conquests. Within a few years, authors [Achebe, Emecheta, Soyinka] addressed more directly and more aggressively aspects of the lives of the colonized that changed due to the presence of the colonizer. Some of these works were, in whole or in part, autobiographical. For women writers in this period, their novels dealt with issues important to them such as the husband-wife/co-wife relationship, the status of the mother/wife, and opportunities for self-development and individuation.

Autobiography

" only the dominant finds his [or her] story worth writing."
Omar Sougou

Writers of autobiography, George Gusdorf posits in Omar Sougou's *Writing Across Cultures,* are generally individuals who, in assessing their personal influence, power, and overall importance because of wealth or ownership, become aware of their individual superiority in acquiring land and controlling people. Omar Sougou, who recounts Susan Stanford Friedman's[2] negative assessment of Gusdorf, states that:

> Autobiographical production would presuppose an acute sense of individual authority and curiosity about oneself. Clearly, in Gusdorf's view awareness of the self emerges from political and ideological conditions among a class of individuals who have asserted their power over others by way of economic opportunity and position. In this manner, then, only the dominant finds his [or her] story worth writing. (30)

The theory is inherently problematic, according to Friedman, since Gusdorf's observations are unable to account for autobiographical texts by women, minorities and writers living in developing countries around the world. Friedman, presenting a counter-argument in Foucauldian terms that argues "the omnipresence of power: not because it embraces everything, but because it comes from everywhere," believes that conditions other than power, authority, and ownership serve to create an atmosphere wherein autobiographical texts might be penned (Foucault, *History of Sexuality* . . . 93). Foucault notes that "where there is power, there is resistance . . . " and Friedman believes that individuals outside of traditional power structures can indeed wield power (*History of Sexuality* . . . 95). She cites "the importance for women and minorities of culturally imposed group identity . . . [and the fact that] critics [do not] sufficiently acknowledge differences in socialization involved in the construction of male and female gender identity" (Sougou 30). Ultimately Friedman asserts that "'the role of collective and relational identities in the individuation of women and minorities' is an important parameter" (Sougou 31). Likewise, James Olney's theory on autobiography suggests a reading of Emecheta's novels. Friedman employs Olney's assertions to identify the origin of the empowerment to write autobiography. Olney writes that autobiography sets forth "a single, radical and radial energy originating in the subject center, an aggressive, creative expression of the self, a defense of individual integrity in the face of an otherwise multiple, confusing, swarming, and inimical universe" (Sougou 31). Sougou believes that "Emecheta's autobiographical writing [is] regarded as a language to articulate self-definition" (32). Emecheta profits from belonging to a culture which values communal interaction and group identity and is empowered through that belonging to proclaim a fully differentiated self. Her autobiographical novels are indeed novels of self-discovery that spring to life because they are rooted in communal realities. For Emecheta, whether it was pure autobiography as presented in her *Head Above Water* or in semi-autobiographical novels such as *Second-Class Citizen* and *In the Ditch*, autobiographical writing was a way to deal with the injustices inextricably linked to her life. In fact, "more than once Emecheta confesses that the exercise [of writing] was therapeutic, 'Writing can be therapeutic and autobiographical writing even more so, as it offers a kaleidoscope view of life'" (Birch 132). It is from this "kaleidoscope view of life" that details spring regarding not only the development and self-culture of a fictional character, but also the development of the author—Emecheta herself.

Emecheta's first two novels chronicle the struggles of Adah Obi, an intelligent and driven young Nigerian who, seeing no other way for self-fulfillment and advancement, follows the tradition of her culture and marries. For African women, marriage and ultimately motherhood guarantee consideration for personhood. Soon thereafter, she finds herself supporting her husband financially from Nigeria while he studies in London. Eventually she joins him there only to learn how he has been transformed by living in the land of the colonizer. Their lives are never the same again, but throughout Adah's struggles raising her children, dealing with her husband and day-to-day life in the metropolitan west, she learns and grows and discovers a self that is proud, honorable and in many ways self-sufficient. Adah eventually leaves her husband and sets up life on her own. She also earns a university degree and becomes a writer. Although *In the Ditch* was written first in 1972, *Second-Class Citizen*, written in 1973, will be considered here first to preserve the chronological narrative as both novels deal with the same characters. After finishing *In the Ditch*, Emecheta decided to tell the beginning of the story in *Second-Class Citizen*.

Second-Class Citizen

Second-Class Citizen lends itself well to a reading as a modern African *Bildungsroman* which chronicles the development of Adah Obi and traces her opportunities, motivations and ultimate individuation. Emecheta's second novel opens with a recollection and a description of what the narrator simply calls a "Presence." The narrator relates that it has never been possible to pinpoint its origin, but that Adah was cognizant of its power around the age of eight. This "Presence," which began "like a dream," is in large part responsible for the personal drive and motivation necessary to better Adah's existence throughout her life (7). Its magical force is referred to multiple times in the first thirty pages of the novel and it soon becomes clear that Adah is propelled by an innate impulse to get an education, grow, and learn about the world and herself. Rita Felski posits that in contemporary female novels of self-discovery[3] the impulse to better oneself generally comes from within. She writes:

> What is important however, and the central characteristic of this kind
> of novel, is that the impulse comes from within; identity is perceived
> as internal rather than socially produced. . . . The novel of self-
> discovery articulates the conviction that the primary obligation for
> women is a recovery of a repressed identity and a consequent refusal
> of social and communal responsibilities which do not accord with in-
> ternal desires. (134-35)

Adah's "Presence" directs her path and guides her in making necessary decisions as she slowly but methodically distances herself from gendered as well as
racially and economically biased existence.

In many ways, Adah profits from being taught early in her life by those
around her. Her informal education, that which comes from her parents and
other relatives, serves as a sort of initial growth and discovery opportunity.
Randolph Shaffner posits that two of the many characteristics of the *Bildungsroman* are that the *Bildungsheld* undergoes some sort of interaction or confron-
tation with his environment and he profits from the lessons of the world (17). It
is clear from the beginning that Adah absorbs much that is said or that goes on
around her. Adah's family now lives in the more cosmopolitan Nigerian capital
of Lagos, but she knows a great deal about Ibuza, her family's native town, because she has paid attention to family discussions:

> Whenever Adah was told that Ibuza was her town, she found it diffi-
> cult to understand. Her parents, she was told, came from Ibuza, and
> so did many of her aunts and uncles. Ibuza, she was told, was a beau-
> tiful town. She had been taught at an early age that the people of
> Ibuza were friendly, that the food there was fresh, the spring water
> was pure and the air was clean. The virtues of Ibuza were praised so
> much that Adah came to regard her being born in a God-forsaken
> place like Lagos as a misfortune. . . . It [Lagos] was bad because it
> was a town with laws,. . . . You had to learn to control your temper,
> which Adah was taught was against the law of nature. (7-8)

Adah's early self-perception is shaped by the comments of her parents. Although Adah's parents teach her and influence her to think about her background in a certain way, they have a hard time deciding whether or not to send
her, their female child, to school. Even though Emecheta emphasizes that the
Ibos value education and formal training, it often remains a difficult decision for
many families whether or not to send their daughters to school. Emecheta admits
that "even if [Adah] went to school, it was very doubtful whether it would be
wise to let her stay long. 'A year or two would do, as long as she can write her
name and count. Then she will learn how to sew.' Adah had heard her mother
say this many many times to her friends" (9). Whether her drive is a result of a
simple thirst for knowledge, a quest for intellect, or whether it is fueled by envy
of her peers attending school and the desire to strike out against the reluctance of
her mother, Adah decides on her own that she must go to school. Emecheta ex-

poses the fact that it is Ma, another female, who stands the strongest against the idea of her daughter's formal education. In *Le deuxième sexe* (1949), Simone de Beauvoir notes that the mother is often the obstacle to her daughter's potential development and, in some cases, her wellbeing. Clearly, several of Emecheta's novels (*The Slave Girl* and *The Joys of Motherhood*) depict the women (mothers and mother figures) in the lives of the various *Bildungshelde* as the ones who try to short circuit available opportunities for self-development. While Beauvoir speaks of the mother's function in universal terms, we must also read Emecheta's texts within a post-colonial context. European colonization brought about such a decomposition of traditional African values that after independence Africans themselves were often complicit in the furtherance of oppressive behaviors toward their own peoples. Ma falls victim to this phenomenon. In short, Ma is always against Adah and over time this creates between Adah and things of the family and home a sort of alienation. Yet, according to Omar Sougou, "[a] quest for self-identity seems to underlie the ensuing diffidence towards home that can be ascribed to the difficult rapport with her mother . . . " (52). Emotional isolation and physical [both parents die while Adah is young] separation from family engender in Adah a self-reliance and determination that eventually facilitate self-definition.

Adah's ingenuity in secretly getting prepared for school is noteworthy. After her decision to go to school is made, she ties a scarf around her waist in order to make her large dress fit better, she slips her Pa's broken slate used for sharpening his razor into her dress so that she might have something on which to write her lessons, and she runs quickly and secretly toward the Methodist School early one afternoon while her mother visits with friends. Adah's creativity and resourcefulness are rewarded when, to her surprise Mr. Cole, the teacher, welcomes her and leads her to a desk in the classroom. Adah proudly claims, "I came to school—my parents would not send me!" (11). After another student shares a section of his pencil with her, "Adah scribbled away, enjoying the smell of craw-craw and dried sweat. She never forgot this smell of school" (11). Adah is so set on getting a formal education that even the threat of canings by her parents does not deter her or distract her from the joy of being in a classroom.

While getting started at her first day of school seems easy enough in the beginning, Adah faces numerous difficulties as she seeks to remain in school and to complete her personal development. Emecheta reminds that "Most dreams, as all dreamers know quite well, do have setbacks. Adah's dream was no exception, for hers had many" (17). One of her first difficulties arises at the end of her first day in the classroom when her Ma realizes that Adah is missing. However, this is not the extent of Adah's tension with Ma. Adah confesses that not only does Ma want to limit her education, but she wants her to learn a useful skill like sewing. It is Ma who canes her the most after learning that she is going to school, it is Ma who "[smacks] and [smacks], and then [nags] and [nags] all day long" (11). Some *Bildung* theorists, Buckley and Labovitz for instance, are quick to note the often-present notion of conflict between generations as an indicative characteristic of the *Bildungsroman*. The individual going through the

Bildungsprozess will in many cases find herself at odds with the guidance and wishes of parents and educators. Here, certainly, it is clear that Adah's firmness of mind stands squarely in the face of her mother's disapproval of the child's chosen path. Later, after her Pa dies, Adah's future schooling is in question since her Ma never encourages her to continue her studies and financial concerns continue to plague the family. Yet Adah is driven by her dream. The "Presence" never leaves her and despite the fact that she often faces seemingly insurmountable obstacles, Adah perseveres.

She continues her formal education, mostly because her mother is advised that the more education Adah receives the higher the bride-price she might bring at her marriage. Pa's death brings about a change of schools and at first, it takes time to adjust to new surroundings. Soon there are threats that Adah might be made to leave school, marry, and help support the family. She grows increasingly concerned about this, so much so that her worries are manifested in her physical features: "The thought of her having to leave school at the end of the year worried her so much that she lost weight. She acquired a pathetically anxious look; the type some insane people have, with eyes as blank as contact lenses" (19). Felski reminds that the process of transformation is never an end to conflict "given the continued reality of a male-governed society; the locus of struggle is however shifted from within the self, in the internalisation of anxiety and guilt, to outside the self, in the struggle between individual and social, female and male demands" (133). Despite continued conflict, her indomitable spirit redeems Adah again and again. At one of her lowest points, both physically and psychologically, Adah's future begins to look more positive:

> At about this time, something happened that showed her that her dream was just suffering a tiny dent, just a small one, nothing deep enough to destroy the basic structure. The dream had by now assumed an image in her mind, it seemed to take life, to breathe and to smile kindly at her. The smile of the Presence became wide as the headmaster of Adah's school announced the lists of available secondary schools which the children could apply for. 'You are going, you must go and to one of the very best of schools; not only are you going, you're going to do well there,' Adah heard the Presence telling her. She heard it so much that she started to smile. (19-20)

Buckley suggests that one of the principal characteristics of traditional *Bildungsromane* is that first experiences in formal education present options not otherwise available to the growing protagonist in a current or former setting (17). Again, while this is a traditional Western *Bildungsroman* characteristic it applies without question to Adah's situation in this African novel. Although it is never easy for her, Adah ultimately expands her mind and her confidence while in the classroom. She takes advantages of opportunities around her as she moves through the various stages of the *Bildungsprozess*.

Like Felski, Abel, Hirsch, and Langland, in their work on fictions of female development, insist that female *Bildungsromane* feature a "heroine's developmental course [that] is more conflicted, less direct . . . " (11). Certainly Adah's path toward self-identity and expansion is never rolled out neatly in front of her. Instead she faces struggles, a voyage of fits and starts, during which she learns much about herself, about the attitudes of those around her, and about her imminent future. Through it all, though, she remains steady, her determination never diminishing. Several examples of such determination serve to illustrate Adah's unique vigor.

Adah, after some reluctance because of an overactive conscience roused by biblical principal, takes two shillings a cousin gives her to buy meat and pays her entrance examination fees for the Methodist Girls' High School. When the truth is found out, Adah receives 103 cane lashings. Nevertheless, it remains clear, even during the caning, that Adah is determined to make something of her life:

> When Cousin Vincent had counted to fifty, he appealed to Adah to cry a little. If only she would cry and beg for mercy, he would let her go. But Adah would not take the bait. She began to see herself as another martyr; she was being punished for what she believed in. . . . After a hundred and three strokes, he told Adah that he would never talk to her again: not in this world nor in the world to come. Adah did not mind that. She was, in fact, very happy. She had earned the two shillings. (21-22)

Adah is determined to ride her "earnings" as far as they would take her. Knowing that scholarship monies go to the students with the top five scores on the examination, Adah "was going to compete for one of those places. She was so determined that not even the fact that her number was nine hundred and forty-seven frightened her. She was going to that school, and that was that!" (22). Adah does win the scholarship plus full room and board and her potential as a fully individuated person, one who experiences authentic selfhood, continues to show itself: "Since [winning the scholarship] she had started to be overawed by the Presence. It existed right beside her, just like a companion. It comforted her during the long school holidays when she could not go home, because there was no home for her to go to" (23). Adah's years at the Methodist Girls' High School go well, if not all too quickly. As her fifth year draws to a close, Adah is faced with making a decision concerning the direction of the next phase of her life.

For Adah marriage seems like the best option. And while getting married is her final decision, it is not a resolution that comes easily. Earlier in the work she vows not to marry and follow traditional Ibo customs that insist that wives be subservient to their husbands (19). Under no circumstances, she once says, will she "consent to live with a husband whom she would have to treat as a master and refer to as "Sir" even behind his back . . . [She] wasn't going to!" (19). However, because of societal expectations for young women, marriage proves her only option after graduation. This decision figures as a sort of personal compromise or sacrifice—for now, Adah would put up with traditional married life, a husband and eventual children, in exchange for consideration as a full-fledged being in her native culture and in hopes of one day arriving at a fully developed and individuated self regardless of that culture. As noted in the Chapter One, Lorna Ellis finds this to be the *modus operandi* of a good many protagonists in female *Bildungsromane*. She suggests that authors of female *Bildungsromane* teach "their protagonists how to understand and work within the limits of their societies . . . [they] allow their heroines to mature or 'grow up'—to understand themselves and their relationship to their environment, and to negotiate that environment in order to maintain some form of agency" (18). According to Ellis "growing down" in time enables "growing up." "She [any female *Bildungsheld*] must give up those aspects of her independence that separate her from patriarchal society, and she must find ways to reconcile her view of herself with others' expectations of her" (Ellis 18). Time and time again, it is evident that Adah, while hidden in plain view, works within the system to define the individual she eventually becomes. Ellis adds that "female *Bildungsromane* offer a limited possibility for female autonomy while simultaneously critiquing the societal expectations that constrict women" (29). Therein lies the impetus of Emecheta's larger project—to critique the African family through its representation in fiction by illustrating common inequalities between husbands and wives as well as the status of women in African and Western societies.

The dynamics of traditional, extended African family politics and "playing the game" in hopes of discovering a developed and individuated self are defining aspects of the "moving to the United Kingdom" episode of the novel. All of her life, Adah has associated life in the United Kingdom with a wonderful, even luxurious, dream life. For her, the words "United Kingdom" suggest so much more than an island nation in Northwest Europe. The narrator relates Adah's impression on hearing those words as a child:

> The title "United Kingdom" when pronounced by Adah's father sounded so heavy, like the type of noise one associated with bombs. It was so deep, so mysterious, that Adah's father always voiced it in hushed tones, wearing such a respectful expression as if he were speaking of God's Holiest of Holies. Going to the United Kingdom must surely be like paying God a visit. The United Kingdom, then, must be like Heaven. (8)

The British Isles, because of Adah's active imagination and the power and mystery they engendered in the minds of many natives of developing countries, are transformed into an attractive destination. What child would not want to see heaven? Abioseh M. Porter suggests too that such a view of the United Kingdom reveals the depths of Adah's naïveté and the extent to which as an adolescent she buys into "[exaggeration] and false conception of Britain" (125). This allure lasts even into adulthood, in fact until she ultimately experiences the harsh realities of "heaven."

After Adah's marriage, she suggests to Francis that they move to London. He could finish a degree in accountancy and after a few months she could join him to work on a degree in librarianship. Adah already has an excellent position at the Amercian library in Lagos so it is assumed that she will stay in Lagos temporarily to save for her fares and those of the children and so that she could continue providing money for Francis's parents and the education of some of his siblings. Thus the plan seems to be falling into place. Initially, Adah sees the opportunity for travel abroad as a means of becoming Ibo élites and the temporary period in Lagos with the children by herself would pass quickly and then she too would become a "been to," an African who has "been to England" (27). However, as Ibo tradition dictates, most family business and decisions must be considered and approved by the husband's parents and according to Francis's parents, Adah is too valuable right where she is. Francis breaks the news to Adah one evening: "Father does not approve of women going to the UK. But you see, you will pay for me, and look after yourself, and within three years, I'll be back. . . . Why lose your good job just to go and see London? They say it is just like Lagos" (28). Adah is infuriated and questions not only the tenets of her traditional culture, but also the insensitivity of her husband. Birch cites Emecheta's explanation concerning the realities of the responsibilities of educated African women:

> In the West, educated women are free and only have themselves to look after. In my country your responsibility increases with your education and wealth. An educated woman has a responsibility to her own family, her husband, and even her own children, who are normally supported by her husband. If I earn a lot of money, I also pay for the education of children who do not form part of my immediate family. (132)

How was Adah to deal with such difficult parents-in-law and a husband who, while he did have an education, still lacked thoughtfulness, sensibility, and common decency? There was nothing else to be done but to feign agreement with the arrangements for now in hopes of one day making it to England in spite of them all:

> So she was to stay in Nigeria, finance her husband, give his parents expensive gifts occasionally, help in paying the school fees for some of the girls, look after her young children and what then, rot? So this was where her great dream had led her. . . . All she had to do was change the situation, and that she was determined to do. She pretended to be all for the plan. Of course, she would stay in Lagos and look after the family; of course she would send him money regularly and, if possible, move in with her mother-in-law. Francis was not to worry about her at all, everything was going to work out well. (28)

Adah reluctantly goes along with the plan and according to Ellis's conception she "grows down" to "grow up." Nonetheless, in her dealings with her husband's family and her own future growth and development, she is resolved to "be as cunning as a serpent but as harmless as a dove" (28).

Travel and seeing the world, according to Shaffner, Howe, and other *Bildung* critics, is an irrefutable requisite for self-expansion and finding one's place in the world. Adah soon devises a plan to leave Lagos and travel to London with the children to see Francis and to experience a new culture. As Adah embarks on this voyage, she is deeply moved and cries "tears of real sorrow at the thought of leaving the land of her birth. . . . It was never going to be the same again. Things were bound to change, for better or worse, but they would never be the same" (34). This proves true in both positive and negative ways.

Although Adah is caught up for a moment in the sorrow of leaving her native land, the atmosphere on the boat quickly causes a change in her focus. She is surrounded by civil servants returning home and the families of diplomats. Indeed for Adah "life was changing fast. Being there, in that first-class section, seemed to give her a taste of what was to come" (34). The trip to England opens up new ways of seeing and experiencing for Adah. She begins it knowing full well that her life is about to undergo a momentous change of direction. Although she admits to being influenced over the years by Western missionaries working in her home country, being in the Western world teaches Adah the good and the bad about her husband, life's realities, and herself. Although she has no way of knowing this because for the present moment everything seems to be falling neatly into place, Adah's life in England will clearly be characterized as "more conflicted, less direct" (Abel, Hirsch, and Langland 11). Adah will continually experience unexpected difficulties which contribute to her *Bildungsprozess*.

Adah's arrival in England is not at all what she might have imagined given what she had been told as a child by Pa about the country. The image of a perfect heaven is quickly replaced with the realities of life in the metropolitan West. The temperate climates of her native Lagos, as well as Takoradi, Freetown, and Las Palmas, ports visited briefly during the voyage, are replaced with the "grey, smoky, and [uninhabited look] "of [a] March day in Liverpool" (36). Right away this seems to be a sort of presage for Adah; her stay in England may not be as "heavenly" as she had anticipated. Additionally, the behavior and appearance of the English she first encounters reflect the unwelcoming weather conditions: "There were hundreds of people rushing around clutching their luggage, and pulling their children, but it was not as noisy as it would have been had they been in Lagos. . . . They looked remote, happy in an aloof way, but determined to keep their distance" (36). Adah accepts her cold welcome and is motivated to make the best of an awkward situation because "her children must have an English education [and she must continue hers] and, for that reason, she was prepared to bear the coldest welcome, even if it came from the land of her dreams. She was a little bit disappointed, but she told herself not to worry. If people like Lawyer Nweze and others could survive it, so could she" (36). Emecheta presents a character imbued with a fantastic sense of survival in the least favorable situations. Adah knows shortly after her reunion with Francis that the West has changed him. He has learned in his few months in the country that they are nothing more than second-class citizens and he quickly shares their status with Adah as she realizes that they will be living in dwellings with uneducated, Nigerian, Indian, Pakistani and West Indian factory workers. She is immediately repulsed by his choice for lodging in London, but Francis

> spat out in anger: 'You must know, my dear young *lady*, that in La-
> gos you may be a million publicity officers for the Americans; you
> may be earning a million pounds a day; you may have hundreds of
> servants: you may be living like an élite, but the day you land in
> England, you are a second-class citizen. So you can't discriminate
> against your own people, because we are all second-class. (39)

Insight regarding her family's new status in British society leaves Adah incredulous. Francis's longing for her to find a simple factory job in order to fit in to the community triggers in her a renewed drive not to settle for such a debased existence. Porter writes that "the protagonist gradually learns that coming to England is not and should not necessarily be the pinnacle of one's dream" (127). Her eyes are slowly opened to the realities of life in her new location and that even some Londoners, like her babysitter Trudy, who keeps a filthy home and carries on a questionable personal life, can be disgusting people.

Adah's reaction to her early experiences in London and her inner recommitment to follow the forceful direction of the "Presence" are characteristics that suggest she is well on her way to self-realization. Shaffner suggests that the successful *Bildungsheld* exhibits qualities of "self-reliance" and "mastery of circumstances" (18). Although she naïvely believes that travel to and relocation in London is to be the life change that will bring instant opportunity, élite status, and overall success, Adah learns quickly that it is not, but more importantly she learns how to deal with the various difficult circumstances she faces. Christina Davis adds: "The fact that Francis himself tells her she is now 'second-class' hastens her toward refusal to capitulate and determined *affirmation of self*" (16). While the degree of success in her growth and development is often qualified and complex, because of her tenacity and affirmative attitude Adah does change and grow in many clear and recognizable ways.

Adah's new job in London presents new opportunities for individuation. On the job, she befriends colleagues from whom she learns a great deal. Being offered such a great position is not only an economic boost for Adah and her family, it also serves to boost her spirits and self-esteem. After such a doubly frigid introduction to life in the West three months before, Adah's new position, which begins in the month of June, warms her to people and recharges her outlook on life's possibilities. Certainly life in London is still mostly difficult, but "she was so proud of her job and so happy on this particular June morning that she found beauty in everything. She saw beauty on the faces of her fellow passengers and heard beautiful sounds from the churning groans of the speeding underground train" (43). Indeed, when Adah is in the "clean, centrally heated library" she feels like she is a first-class citizen (45). In many other places and on other occasions, however, Adah senses tensions and difficulties which challenge her to the core.

Feminist [or womanist or stiwanist or Motherist[4]] ideologies are an overarching concern of Emecheta's *œuvre* and as such have been discussed by many critics from numerous perspectives. Without a doubt, *Second-Class Citizen* serves as a sort of forum for protest for Emecheta. Lloyd W. Brown notes that "with Emecheta the fervor and rhetoric of protest –that is, the explicit and unequivocal denunciation of the sexual status quo—have not diminished" (35). But again Emecheta's works have only a few things in common with those of Western feminist writers and theorists. Katherine Fishburn addresses the "dialogic heteroglossia" of Emecheta's novels noting that Westerners often misinterpret her novels due to the inability to fully grasp the interworkings and nuances of a foreign culture (44). Fishburn proposes a Bakhtinian reading of Emecheta's works. In *The Dialogic Imagination*, Bakhtin suggests that,

> at any given moment of its evolution, language is stratified not only into linguistic dialects in the strict sense of the word, . . . but also—and for us this is the essential point—into languages that are socio-ideological: languages of social groups, 'professional' and 'generic' languages, languages of generations and so forth. From this point of view, literary language itself is only one of these heteroglot languages—and in its turn is also stratified into languages (generic, period-bound and others). (271-72)

Fishburn believes that a clear and more valid interpretation of a work of African origin is possible when Western readers are aware of and filter their readings of a given alien text through this concept of "ideologically saturated" language (qtd in Fishburn 44). Granted, *Second-Class Citizen* (as well as most of Emecheta's other novels) seemingly aligns itself, oftentimes seamlessly, with traditional Western feminist discourse. I propose, however, based on the work of Fishburn and others, that while there appears on the surface to be much in common with Western feminism much more is at stake in this novel. Adah's conjugal experiences as well as her involvement in incidents related to home life mature her and allow her to arrive at a qualified state of self-development and individuation. Home life for Adah and her family is overwhelmingly difficult at best. Francis's nature in general and the changes in personality he undergoes after spending time in London constantly cause hardship and tension for the marriage relationship. Nonetheless, Adah is able to meet the challenges of her home life and general surroundings with reasonable success.

From her first night in England, Adah experiences conjugal discord because of her tyrannical husband. Days after her arrival, she discovers that she is pregnant with their third child. Not only does the new pregnancy give her peaceful nights, but it and its associated marital conflict make her determined more than ever to land a job that would give her excellent professional experience and help support her family. Even though the job requires a medical examination during which the fact that she is expecting a baby would be exposed, Adah passes with flying colors and learns a great deal in the process. Concerning her doctor's visit for the medical exam, she learns that sometimes honesty is not the best policy. Likewise, Adah comes to realize that Francis would not leave her even though he might be quite upset about her pregnancy because "she was still laying the golden eggs. . . . As before, her pay bound him to her but the difference was that she now knew it" (42). Faced with adversity, Adah is true to her African upbringing which taught her "very early to be responsible for herself. Nobody was interested in her for her own sake, only in the money she would fetch, and the housework she could do and Adah, happy about being given this opportunity of survival, did not waste time thinking about its rights and wrongs. She had to survive" (18). Assuming responsibility for herself, Adah continues her *Bildungsprozess*.

The fact that Adah generally still cares for Francis and wants him to succeed in his studies and in life in spite of his egregious and inexcusable mistreatment of her is noteworthy. She does not pin the blame for her own challenges on his actions and behaviors, which themselves constitute some of the worst effects of colonization. Both are victims of dreadful circumstances; yet as mentioned earlier in this chapter, the cohesion of the African family through even the worst of times takes priority. With confidence, Adah not only becomes the family's breadwinner, but its leader and backbone. Emecheta writes of the pity that Adah, in a sense, feels for her husband. Her willingness to do more than her share demonstrates her developing maturity and that she is coming into her own as a fully individuated person:

> Looking back at that time, she still wondered why she never thought it odd that she should be doing all the worrying about what they were going to live on, why she, and she alone, always felt she was letting those she loved down if she stayed away from work, even for the sake of having a baby. The funniest thing was that she felt it was her duty to work, not her husband's. He was to have an easy life, the life of a mature student, studying at his own pace. (95)

After all, "Francis was not a bad man, just a man who could no longer cope with the overdemanding society he found himself in" (101). Although Emecheta reveals that Francis never really made a decision on his own even in Africa, when he relocates to the West, Francis finds himself in surroundings wherein his agency is all the more erased.

In his *Peau Noire, Masques Blancs* (*Black Skin, White Masks*), psychiatrist Frantz Fanon identifies certain patterns of behavior that are the products of extended colonization. This study on the psychology of racism and colonial oppression along with his second text *Les damnés de la terre* (*The Wretched of the Earth*) claim that colonization succeeded at shifting the mindset of Africans from pride and independence to inferiority and domination. And that even after independence, Africa drowns in neo-colonialism wherein the élite African leaders (the *comprador* class) simply take the place of the white colonizers who have returned home. The new African leaders ensure that daily business runs as it had during colonization. Consequently, no real change in structure or function of rule takes place. Francis feels the brunt of these invisible, yet absolutely real forces and he suffers from what the narrator calls a blackness of the mind. Emecheta diagnoses the situation:

> Even if Francis did qualify [academically], he would never have the courage to bring her to a restaurant to eat, not in London anyway, because he firmly believed that such places were not for blacks. Adah knew that his blackness, his feeling of blackness, was firmly established in his mind. She knew that there was discrimination all over the place, but Francis's mind was a fertile ground in which such attitudes could grow and thrive. (57-8)

It is Adah alone who over time learns to deal with such psychological mind games. She remains strong and determined as she stays the course toward self-development. She truly has eyes to see more, she will not settle for such a mundane existence.

In the course of what appears outwardly as one of the lowest points in her life in London, Adah makes her own decisions. Her experiences in the maternity ward when she is hospitalized to give birth to her third child enlighten Adah. Adah feels that she is an oddity in this setting not only because Francis does not openly express his love and concern for her like the other husbands, but for several other reasons as well. She is physically marginalized in the maternity ward as "she was on the bed at the extreme end . . . , next to the door" (110). She is all too aware that her bedside table is empty while her wardmates' tables overflow with cards, photos and flowers. Although all the women in the ward are recovering from giving birth, Adah feels ashamed of her continued bleeding and that she is the only patient wearing the common hospital gown. In the hospital, Adah has much time to think. During the doctors' rounds she wants so much to open up to them, to express her internalized and overwhelming need to be an individual, a person who matters for once. In one instance, Adah starts to cry as the doctors begin their examination. They dismiss her emotions as "after-baby blues" (115). The reality of the situation demonstrates in a microcosmic glimpse one of the principal purposes of Emecheta's novel:

> She did not want to stop [crying] because she might be tempted to babble the truth to [the doctors]. She might be tempted to tell them that for once in her whole life she hated being what she was. Why was it she could never be loved as an individual, the way the sleek woman was being loved, for what she was and not just because she could work and hand over money like a docile child? Why was it that she was not blessed with a husband like that woman who had had to wait for seventeen years for the arrival of her baby son? The whole world seemed so unequal, so unfair. Some people were created with all the good things ready-made for them, others were just created like mistakes. God's mistakes. (115)

Personal development and organic wholeness is Adah's long held wish. From the push by the "Presence" to get a formal education in order to make something of herself to manipulating her extended family to be able to settle in London to facing the few highs and abundant lows of living in the colonizers' culture, Adah remains relatively focused on her personal growth and development.

While her traditional Ibo culture prizes family and communal life, something to which Adah, despite the difficulties it has brought, clings even during the difficult days in London, it is in the hospital that Adah finally ponders the eventual possibility that she might be better off without Francis. Clearly, he is shown to be physically and mentally abusive toward Adah, so getting away from him seems reasonable. Seeing him, perhaps for the first time, as a sort of necessary evil, but undeniable liability to her self-development, Adah considers "switching her love" to her children. She could "*leave this person. No, live with him as long as it is convenient. No longer*" (122). Sooner than she thinks, it will no longer be "convenient." Adah understands that she had looked for her home, the place she could find comfort and grow "in the wrong place and among the wrong people. That did not mean the whole world was wrong or that she could never start another home. . . . She would not harm [Francis], because he was the father of her babies. But he was a dangerous man to live with. Like all such men, he needed victims. Adah was not going to be a willing victim" (122). These realizations serve as yet another moment of awakening for this *Bildungsheld* and can be read not only in the context of this one woman's relationship with her husband, but analogously as an insightful comment on the relationship between the colonizer and the colonized. Adah is always in the process of growing toward self-fulfillment. Having eyes to see more, she never settles for long in situations wherein she is not allowed to express herself as a full person.

A last lesson Adah learns in the hospital, and one that will ultimately reward her in the future, centers on the importance of expressing thanks and appreciation to those who do things for her. Adah recognizes from her time in the maternity ward that had she been thoughtful and appreciative instead of focussing on her own dismal conditions vis-à-vis the other patients, that she might not have been so miserable. Committing to the future expression of heartfelt appreciation and social graciousness, to speak out and connect with people instead of focusing solely on personal circumstances, is a decision not to remain an "other." Instead Adah attempts to find her own sort of agency, to become a participant in social discourse, and to develop her individuated self. Such experience, especially that pertaining to a deep consciousness of human experience and necessity of self-expression, is the essence of the traditional *Bildungsroman* (Shaffner 18).

After the turmoil surrounding the birth of her third child, Adah asserts herself in the hopes that she can prevent future children. When Francis learns that she has forged his signature on a document permitting her to obtain a vaginal cap, he humiliates her in front of their neighbors. When the situation becomes unbearable, their landlord sends the inquisitive neighbors away; but more importantly, Adah realizes that life with Francis is categorically over:

> Her marriage with Francis? It was finished as soon as Francis called
> in the Nobles and the other tenants. She told herself that she could not
> live with such a man. Now everybody knew she was being knocked
> about, only a few weeks after she had come out of the hospital. Eve-
> rybody knew that the man she was working for and supporting was
> not only a fool, but that he was too much of a fool to know that he
> was acting foolishly. (147)

No more will she support financially or in any other fashion his lazy inattention
to matters important to the family, his constant TV watching, his insensitivity or,
most seriously, his beatings. After learning the news that she is expecting her
fourth child, Adah worries about Francis's reactions and asks her doctor to help
her terminate the pregnancy. Emecheta writes:

> She now saw this situation as a challenge, a new challenge. When she
> was little and alone, the challenge had been that of educating herself,
> existing through it all, alone, all by herself. She had hoped that in
> marriage she could get herself involved in her man's life and he
> would share the same involvement in hers. . . . Now she was alone
> again with this new challenge that included her children as well. She
> was going to live, to survive to exist through it all. . . . She was be-
> coming aware of the Presence again—the Presence that had directed
> her through childhood. She went nearer to It in her prayers . . . she
> talked to Him when she woke up in the morning; she talked to Him
> all the time, and Adah felt that He was always there. (150)

Adah gradually grows away from her husband. All the while, she appears to lead
a more spiritualized existence. Felski suggests that the novel of self-discovery
"typically depicts a process of separation as the means to defining identity, set in
motion through an act of departure; it traces a development of self-knowledge
either in isolation, in nature, or in the female community" (135). As is disclosed
in *In the Ditch*, the narrative sequel to *Second-Class Citizen*, Adah's escape
finds her temporarily living in Pussy Cat Mansions, which is in essence a female
community.

    Near the end of *Second-Class Citizen*, Adah leaves Francis for good. This
rupture in their relationship is the "separation as the means to defining identity"
to which Felski refers (135). Adah's departure opens up for her new opportunities for self-development and growth. Brown reminds us that this is a close call
for Adah: "she is in danger of becoming a second-class citizen in the most crucial sense of the term—in the sense of personal direction and independent self-
awareness. She almost lacks the initiative to break out of a marriage which is
destroying her emotional and physical resources, and only does so after her husband nearly beats her to death" (47-8). While nothing is ever easy for a Nigerian female living in London, Adah faces her challenges head on and always
makes the best of difficult situations.

    For a long time, she tells us, Adah has wished to become a writer. With four
children, a dependent and difficult husband, and other domestic responsibilities,

it is almost impossible to imagine this woman having the time to write a novel. Nonetheless, this is what Adah does. She carves out three hours during her already busy afternoons and she writes. The narrator relates that "the more she wrote, the more she knew she could write and the more she enjoyed writing. She was feeling this urge: *Write, go on and do it, you can write*" (161). Adah's finished product is not much more than over-romanticized "scenes with sickly adolescent love sentiments" (164). Yet, she has written a book; she has poured herself into a project, *The Bride Price*, which relates all of the feeling and emotion missing in her conjugal relationship. Brown recalls the perseverance Adah displays her whole life. From her determination to get an education early on, her calculated decision to seek a better life for herself and her family and ultimately to leaving her husband, Adah is quite aware of the direction in which she is headed. All of her actions "evince the survival of that strong-willed independence that has always motivated her" (Brown 48). More importantly Brown asserts that her "ability to survive and to sustain her will is an essentially creative talent, one that is analogous to the creative resources of the artist" (48). This is important for two reasons.

First, it is important because it points to yet another critical characteristic of the *Bildungsroman*. The realities of life for certain Africans in colonial and postcolonial periods involve struggles for simple survival and self-preservation, all the more for African women. If a Nigerian woman can display "an essentially creative talent" in her struggle to survive not to mention even thrive in the social context of the metropolitan West, she demonstrates remarkable progress toward individual self-expansion and self-definition. It is important to recall that Shaffner, referring to characteristics of the traditional *Bildungsroman*, cites "the idea that *living is an art* which the apprentice may learn" and that "a young person can become adept in the *art of life*" (18, emphasis added). Certainly, Adah's existence is oftentimes more struggle than simple "living," a fact which makes her ultimate successes, her display of creative talent in and through struggle, all the more extraordinary.

Second, Brown likens Adah's creative mastery of the social circumstances of everyday life in London to the creative abilities of an artist (48). It is more than fitting, notes Brown, that Adah becomes a writer. Thus, not only does she become an appropriately socialized and balanced individual albeit in a qualified sense; a process accomplished with artistic flair, but she also is able to showcase the more traditional artistic talents through her storytelling. Bill, Adah's coworker at the Chalk Farm Library, describes *The Bride Price* as her fifth child, an indisputable brainchild that arrives after tumultuous gestation and difficult labor. Brown synthesizes the significance of this episode in terms of Adah's overall path to ultimate enlightenment and expansion:

> In keeping with Emecheta's penchant for establishing pointed analogies, the second-class status of being African, female, and poor is counterbalanced by a second set of analogies which constitute a "first-class" capacity for independence and creativity—Adah's pride

and ambitions as a student, her protective strength as a mother, and now a newly discovered talent that seems to be another version of motherhood. . . . In fact Adah's writing has become more than an analogy, it is an act of self-affirmation, proclaiming that inner resourcefulness that refuses to accept the status of second-class citizen. (48)

When Francis spitefully burns the manuscript to *The Bride Price*, he, essentially, kills Adah's child. Emecheta has already revealed Francis's lack of faith in himself to ever finish his studies, thus it becomes evident that Francis has decided that if he is not going to be successful then he is going to do his utmost to keep Adah from experiencing any sort of success. Quoting from Susan Suleiman[5], Porter acknowledges that "in almost all [novels of development], there is always at least one character who, instead of helping the protagonist, will serve as an impediment to the latter's progress. . . . It is . . . clear that Francis . . . is her leading 'opposant' or opponent" (127). Despite Francis's antagonism, Adah is helped by a good many people along the way as well. Mrs. Konrad, Mr. Okpara and her co-worker, Bill console and encourage Adah. Suleiman calls these individual helpers or guides on the path to development "adjuvants" (Porter 128-29). Adah decides that for her own survival and that of her children, she must leave Francis. *Second-Class Citizen* concludes with Adah's final proclamation of hope in the face of turmoil stirred up by Francis. In the wake of what amounts to Francis's disowning of his offspring, Adah is determined that her eyes will indeed see the light of a better day and an expanded existence for herself and her soon-to-be five children.

Notes

1 For more information on distinctions between Western feminism and African feminism and varieties of African feminism please consult Chapters 1-5 of Susan Arndt's *The Dynamics of African Feminism*, Trenton, NJ: Africa World Press, 2002.
2 Susan S. Friedman, "Women's Autobiographical Selves, Theory and Practice." in *The Private Self: Theory and Practice of Women's Autobiographical Writings*, ed. Shari Benstock (London: Routledge, 1988): 34-62.
3 Felski's article "The Novel of Self Discovery A Necessary Fiction?" focuses on Western literature and while Western and African literature do not share all literary and aesthetic characteristics, this one in particular seems to apply to this African text.
4 See Susan Arndt's *The Dynamics of African Feminism: Defining and Classifying African Feminist Literatures*. Africa World Press, 2002.
5 See Suleiman's "La Structure d'apprentissage" in *Poétique*, vol. 37 1979, pp. 24-42. Suleiman's paradigm is based on the work of Souriau and Propp.

Chapter 3

"you're always out, aren't yer?": Self – Development Progresses in Emecheta's *In the Ditch*

> *"But one thing about which [Adah] was determined was that she was not going to lower herself anymore for anything. The world had a habit of accepting the way you rated yourself. The last place in which she was going to incarcerate herself was in the ditch."* Buchi Emecheta, *In the Ditch*

Although written first, *In the Ditch* is the narrative sequel to *Second-Class Citizen*. *In the Ditch* follows Adah Obi's (and Emecheta's) story from her move with her children out of the home she shared with her husband Francis through a stay at the Pussy Cat Mansions and ultimately to the Matchboxes, a flat across from Regent's Park in London. It is in *In the Ditch* that Adah undergoes some of her fiercest trials as she takes care of and provides for her five children while continuing her studies before she gives in to the system briefly with the insight that things will eventually be better. There are without a doubt many feverishly desperate and hopeless days spent "in the ditch." Yet through her experiences, Adah learns much about her individual role within social and interpersonal dynamics allowing her finally, after much indecision and fear, to grow and become her own person. After leaving Francis, Adah does not just curl up and wither away. On the contrary, she continues to gather new knowledge and wisdom, as she had done since primary school, from careful observation of situations played out around her. One such striking realization comes just after Adah has moved into a room rented from a fellow Nigerian. Realizing he can take advantage of Adah's straits, the landlord refuses to respond to Adah's request to exterminate filthy rodents and cockroaches, charges her double the rent of similar sized rooms in that neighborhood, and tries to scare her senseless by dressing up as a juju, a supernatural being or evil spirit. In the face of such hardship, Adah reaches deep down and seemingly becomes stronger. Instead of playing into the hands of the landlord and succumbing to his taunts and intimidation, Adah, keeping her uncommon, level-headed wits about her, shows no fear. Emecheta chronicles her reflection on the matter:

> Why was it that she was not afraid? she wondered. Was it because here in England one's mind was always taken up with worrying about the things that really matter? But juju mattered to her at home in Nigeria all right; there, such a scene in the middle of the night could even mean death for some. Probably, she thought, it was because there it was the custom, the norm, and what everybody believed in. . . . But here, in north-west London, how could she think of the little man who was so familiar to her by day . . . as a medicine man? (3)

While Adah recalls hearing of or reading about other Nigerians in London who are "being 'terrorised' by juju," she is not in the least bit frightened (3). Katherine Fishburn adds that "being in England seems to have given Adah the strength to withstand what would otherwise be a seductively compelling perspective" (53). In the context of London, the juju seems silly and excessive. While life in the United Kingdom is far from the heavenly paradise those words connoted in her youth, the place does serve as a milieu wherein Adah can develop a certain empowerment and freedom. In the final analysis, this personal strength serves her well. For it is after a time in England that Adah exclaims: "I am tough and free, . . . free . . . " and "in England, anything could be tried, and even done. It's a free country" (3, 5). Those freedoms include not having to fear a tyrannical landlord playing juju, knowing that, even though the process at times proves agonizing, one eventually is able to find agreeable housing and other provisions, and not having to remain in a destructive conjugal relationship.

Throughout the novel, Emecheta expounds upon the racial situation as it exists in London. In fact, in Chapter One, when reflecting on the absurdity of her landlord's deviant portrayal of a juju, Adah is infuriated at how the spectacle is perceived by unsuspecting neighbors. In what amounts to a Fanonian Manichean interpretation of the situation, Adah wonders what "picture they, the Nigerians, must present to their neighbors. . . . Who told them that the Devil was black? Who told them that angels were always white? Had it never occurred to them that there might be black angels and a white devil?" (5). The negative and backward manner in which Africans are almost always perceived by Westerners is precisely one of the things Adah intends to combat in her quest for self-development. In this incident Adah "reclaimed a racial loyalty" as she ponders the stereotypical perceptions Westerners most likely have of Africans (Fishburn 56). While Adah does find new opportunity and new ways of seeing in London, she is also reminded of the things that make her own culture distinctive and valuable. Later, Fishburn cites Myra Jehlen's claims concerning the "organically individualistic" quality of the Western novel: "On her view, the novel is structured around 'the unitary self versus the others'; it is additionally 'about the generation, the becoming, of that self'" (58). If the African novel is generally to be considered antithetical to the Western novel; in other words, a novel featuring loyalty to the community instead of individualism, how is it possible that a protagonist might break free from her difficult husband, from the wishes of their extended family, from oppressive and degrading expectations of women, from the deceiving warmth of a community of female tenants at the Mansions to grow and develop into a coherent individual?   Lloyd Brown offers this perspective:

> Emecheta's contention is that even in the most unpromising circumstances the individual never really loses the potential for choice and strength, and it is crucial to note that Adah manages to continue her education (despite formidable obstacles) because she is determined to escape the slum and its humiliations. Thus, it remains the individual's ultimate responsibility, even in the most unlikely circumstances, to develop what is essentially an indestructible strength of will—as Emecheta perceives it. (43)

Emecheta often exposes the complexities that arise when divergent cultures intermingle.

In *Second-Class Citizen*, we recall that Francis is quick to tell Adah that in her move to the West, she should become accustomed to social and racial inferiority. And while in time Adah senses exactly that, she struggles to avoid relegation to such subordinate status. *In the Ditch* exposes similar kinds of prejudice, but Adah now must face them on her own without a husband—a status, Emecheta reminds us, that remains taboo in Nigeria. She must live on the dole and in the slums with five dependent children in tow. After she moves to the run down, thin-walled community called Pussy Cat Mansions, Adah bears the brunt of not so subtle insults from her neighbors, the Small family. On one occasion, just a few days after Adah's arrival at the Mansions, Mr. Small knocks loudly on her door to ask that she and her children not make so much noise. He begins the conversation without an introduction yet he assures Adah that "[he doesn't] mind [her] colour!" (18). Stunned, Adah quickly realizes the color to which he is referring is the color of her skin.

While awkward racial tensions subtly lace *In the Ditch*, the salient issue becomes economic and gendered. Adah, a single mother, has joined a diverse community of mostly single mothers. What is working against these "problem families," to insure that they remain in subordinate positions, finds its origin in the welfare system of English society. Sougou acknowledges:

> Life at Pussy Cat Mansions (the ditch) would exemplify the marginalization of immigrants living in the "anomie or classlessness" which they share with underprivileged British natives and women. The novel charts personal experience; it is written in some respects from a social-science graduate's perspective. This appears clear from the attention paid to the plight of the Mansion dwellers and to the working of the welfare system. (33)

In time, it is suggested that Carol, the Mansions' on-site social worker and seemingly good-hearted advocate for the down and out, along with the rest of the bureaucrats at the head of the welfare administration may be to blame for difficulties the ditch dwellers have escaping their desperate conditions. While talking with a fellow sociologist, Adah realizes that "People like Carol were employed to let them know their rights, but the trouble was that Carol handed them their rights, as if she was giving out charity" (98). The actions of those employed by the welfare system thus appear to become vestiges of colonial imperialism—perhaps a contorted version of Kwame Nkrumah's neo-colonialism[1]. Adah's quest for self-definition and self-development leads her through the difficult days at Pussy Cat Mansions. She does indeed "grow down" as she climbs the seemingly endless, filthy steps to her flat each day; yet Adah manages by the end of the novel to pull herself out of the ditch. Although for a while, she becomes quite comfortable in the midst of the squalor and chaos of the Mansions, after all, misery *and poverty* love company; however, she is never blinded by or completely consumed by all that goes on around her. Although she does not mention the "Presence" that once guided her, it is as if it is there subconsciously helping her to see her way out of the destitution and toward individual self-realization. Sougou suggests that "*In the Ditch* explores Adah's insecurity and the support of the female community, the process of 'othering,' the pursuit of self-definition, and finally, blackness, Africa and Africans" (33). Though it takes her far out of her comfort zone and causes her much anguish as she parts with neighbors who have become good friends and co-sufferers, Adah finds the requisite inner resolve and the outside help to bring herself and her children out of the Mansions. Another stage in her *Bildungsprozess* is complete.

Once a flat had been located, the choice to move to the Pussy Cat Mansions is an easy one for Adah. She is so ready to move away from her opportunistic and threatening landlord that any place, no matter how awful, seems inviting. Despite its prison-like appearance, its squalid and dangerous stairways and the fact that it was built over an old cemetery, Adah is quick to accept her own flat at the compound. The first night there, Adah and her children sleep on the floor. They do not yet have the necessary items to set up their new home, but Adah knows "there were three important things . . . she had acquired that night, her independence, her freedom, and peace of mind" (15). It is somewhat counterintuitive to declare this move the first step toward Adah's individuation and self-sufficiency because of the new and equally daunting predicaments in which she finds herself. However, Adah proves, in Ellis's conception, that it is often necessary to "grow down" in order to "grow up" (18, 29). Ironically, after a few days and Mr. Small's rude request, Adah in fact finds her new community quite warm and nourishing. She grows accustomed to the banality of her fellow dwellers' actions and language. Being around others in the similar circumstances of single parenthood and immigrant status serves a therapeutic purpose. Sougou notes that "the closeness of the female ditch-dwellers plays a major part in the struggle against insecurity and for self-definition" (34). Adah is not only close to her fellow Mansion dwellers, but she befriends Carol who goes to great lengths to help out the family.

Carol arranges for sitters for the children through the Family Task Force so that Adah can continue her evening studies. Later, when Carol confronts the young mother about leaving her children too early in the morning at the school sheds, Adah resigns herself to the fact that she must quit her job in order to take proper care of her children. Along with her job resignation comes the stark realization that she is sinking deeper in the ditch:

> Her socialisation was complete. She, an African woman with five children and no husband, no job, and no future, was just like most of her neighbours—shiftless, rootless, with no rightful claim to anything. . . . That closed her middle-class chapter. She couldn't claim to be working class, because the working class had a code for daily living. Joblessness baptised her into the Mansions' society. . . . She joined the ditch-dwellers' association. She joined the mothers' local socials. She resigned herself to the mysterious inevitability and accepted things as they were. . . . She was comforted by the warmth of [. . .] acceptance, and was thankful. (31-2)

Adah's slow but sure descent into the world of unemployment and poverty is made complete when she is convinced to go on the dole. Accepting public assistance monies strips Adah of her pride and reminds her that she has become one of those "lazy, parasitic people who lived off Society" (33). Perhaps even worse than her loss of pride and sense of self worth in accepting the funds is that her "dream of being an author had vaporized" (33). Becoming an author has the potential of being one of the most important steps in Adah's *Bildungsprozess*.

With the upheaval of moving to the Mansions, getting her children settled, getting to know quirky neighbors and quitting her job, Adah is unable to focus fully on the quality of her writing and consequently receives several rejection slips for short stories she submits for publication. Yet it is critical to note that even the morning Adah decides to register for welfare, she senses that she will eventually grow through these tribulations. She is at once cognizant of the fact that she must have the means to live in the present and is hopeful that the future will bring freedom from the bonds of public assistance: "'I may not have to be on the dole for long,' she thought. 'I may still become a writer, a writer of a best selling book, I may still become a qualified social scientist who may one day be an advisor like Carol. Meanwhile, I must live, and I must look after the kids that God gave me alive" (34). Becoming a successful writer or a degreed social assistant would indicate that Adah had attained, at least in the professional arena, a heightened level of formation and development. She remains hopeful for such a day.

While in the Dole House, Adah begins a conversation of general small talk about Africa and Africans with a white woman. The conversation triggers in Adah contemplation on what it means for Nigerians to be truly successful in England. Adah admits that fellow Nigerians often insist on being married in the nicest of places while living in London; likewise, some even insist on having "a real red carpet for their weddings" (37). Granted, Adah was enraptured before leaving Lagos by all that the "kingdom of heaven" might make available to her in terms of privilege and material possessions; yet her desires for "been to" or élite status become tempered by the realities of living day to day in a place so permeated with gender, racial, and economic status biases. Adah's definition of success is quickly altered. She refuses to define success in terms of being like those opportunistic Nigerians who were "from a country where kids still died from malnutrition, where three-quarters of the population had never tasted clean tap water, where there were still all sorts of horrors arising from illiteracy, yet where they, the so-called enlightened ones, blew what little money they had on [. . .] extravagances" (37). After being confronted by a man selling glass birds on the street, Adah ponders the utter ridiculousness of someone like her buying such ornamentation: "'Poor old man, standing there all day and asking people like me to buy a glass bird. What would I do with a beautiful thing like that? Where would I put it? The dole money will just do to keep me and my five alive. Buy a bird indeed!' said Adah seriously" (45). Adah's selfhood transformations, unlike those of most of her compatriots, are not pretentious or superficial. She understands what is most important in her development and what will ultimately serve her and her family well.

At no point does Adah claim that becoming a writer would propel her above others in terms of worth. At no point does she exhibit any lasting form of resentment as a byproduct of the abysmal circumstances she finds while living in the West. Indeed, she refuses to accept second-class status and fights often to keep from being relegated to that position by others, yet that stems not from self-righteous indignation, but from a universal sense of justice and equality. Some may point out that Adah shirks her responsibilities of motherhood in order to pursue selfish goals when she leaves her five children in the Mansions alone in the evenings to attend classes. Carol later informs her that leaving children unattended in London constitutes parental negligence. However, leaving her children alone for the evening is what Adah would have innocently done had she been living in Lagos. On the contrary, Adah's self-development and formation is carried out with selfless aims so that not only she can attempt to escape the oppressive circumstances that have plagued her since childhood, but so that her children can, as well.

Adah's descent into the ditch ironically places her in an environment of warmth and camaraderie. Living in London, the seat of the former colonizers, magnifies Adah's weaker attributes. She admits "she always felt insecure, uncertain and afraid. It is a curse to be an orphan, a double curse to be a black one in a white country, an unforgivable calamity to be a woman with five kids but without a husband" (70-1). But with so many things working against her, Adah does find some security in her life at the Mansions. Adah gets to know several of the key dwellers there such as Whoopey and her mother Mrs. Cox, Mrs. O'Brien and the Princess. She joins the Tenants' Association on the insistence of Mrs. Ashley and eventually becomes an admired and respected tenant. For Mrs. O'Brien, whose family receives more income on public assistance than when her husband actually works a job, Adah becomes a friendly ear and sounding board. She reminds the Irish immigrant that feeding her children is more important than the neighbors' verbal jabs about a lazy husband. And even though Mrs. O'Brien offends Adah by stereotypically grouping her with "her people," in other words, other Africans, Adah ignores the comment because "she sensed that the O'Brien woman was feeling low and was begging for understanding" (47). To varying degrees, racial issues do arise on occasion at the Mansions. Adah, however, has cultivated a healthy way of working through such blatant racism. Nonetheless, there is one white neighbor named Whoopey who seems to be blind to racial differences.

Whoopey is a constant source of advice and reassurance for Adah. Always well connected to the goings-on at the Mansions, Whoopey, on one occasion, is the first to let Adah know that a new delivery of used clothing has just arrived at Carol's office. She tells Adah to go quickly in order to find good things for her children. When Adah is expecting a visit by Public Ministry men to assess their need for new shoes, Whoopey advises Adah not to have her flat too warm so that the officials think she can always afford such luxury. Finally, it is Whoopey who insists that Adah complain about menacing dogs that use her front door as a toilet. Whoopey, schooled in the fine art of surviving in the Mansions, coaches Adah in the appropriate ways of handling certain situations: "You don't shout loud enough, that's your trouble. I'll do the shouting for you. Those dogs must be stopped" (68). Whoopey's obstinacy ignites in Adah a short-lived determination to demand that the filthy situation be taken care of before she pays her rent. The clerk suggests that something will be done, but first, Adah must pay. As Adah is about to give in, another white tenant in line behind her pulls Adah's hand back and they all join forces to demand that action be taken. Such a demand along with the refusal to pay certainly catches the clerks off guard: "The other clerks had now stopped work and simply stared at the two white women with a black one sandwiched in between like a good sponge cake. Differences in culture, colour, backgrounds and God knows what else had all been submerged in the face of greater enemies—poverty and helplessness" (71). The ditch dwellers, diverse in terms of race, level of education and individual challenges, create a unified front against rampant injustice. The Mansions provide a context for "a warm chat, a nice cup of tea and solidarity against any foe" (71). Up against the clerks and demanding that something be done about her situation, "[Adah] felt strong, and even crossed her arms akimbo and threw her tightly-scarved head back. *It's a free country*, her attitude seemed to say" (71). Sadly, even though Adah's complaint is written in "the book" and the women are promised that it would be looked into, nothing is ever really done. Although Adah learns from her neighbors and grows as an individual because of her interaction with them, she knows that as for her life in the West it will be "very difficult to change anything" (72). She has faced so much rejection and injustice that, for a period at least, Adah feels more inclined to shrink from difficult circumstances than face them directly. It appears that Adah has lost her drive for individuation and self-expansion.

While it is obvious that the communal bonds created between the Mansions' residents are strong and comforting, it also becomes obvious that soon everyone would be made to move. The thought of such an upheaval in her life sends cold blood through Adah's veins. She had become so accustomed to the support of those around her. No, life had never been easy in the ditch, but at least she was not alone. Emecheta describes her protagonist's fears:

> [Adah] was a regular reader of *New Society*, and some other social science magazines. She was not unaware of a few social theories. But the situation that was working itself out at the Pussy Cat Mansions fitted into no such theories. As a sort of community had worked itself into being, everybody knew the business of everybody else. That sort of life suited her. There was always a friend to run to in time of trouble. . . . To go to a new area now seemed as formidable as going to a new country. Most tenants at the Pussy felt differently; they looked forward to the change. They had their relatives living nearby, so they did not have to depend on community life like Adah. (87-8)

Adah now knows what the citizens in those young countries in Africa must have felt like facing independence: "When they got their independence, they found that it was a dangerous toy" (95). The Mansions represent in microcosm the ordeals and dilemmas many newly independent African countries went through.

While listening to Whoopey's sister Peggy expound upon Carol's faults as well as the general failings of the welfare system, Adah decides with renewed resolution that she will face her future. Exposure to the Cox family's perspective on the welfare system teaches Adah a lesson—"One thing was apparent, thought Adah, [Peggy] did not like the situation she found herself in. Unlike [her sister] Whoopey she was never going to accept that situation from society. She would fight to pull herself out of the ditch. Adah learned a lesson from her. She too, would like to face her own world" (95). Brown contends that

> Emecheta has made her point in Adah's last-minute recognition of her own responsibilities to herself. Notwithstanding the need to de-

nounce the destructiveness of external systems, and without minimizing the value of sisterhood among the mums of her world, the ultimate solution rests with the individual woman alone, for she must recapture the initiative and restore the inner strength that has been sapped by poverty and institutionalized dependency. (43)

Resolved to move forward with her life and for the sake of her children's lives, Adah accepts the fact that a change of living arrangements is necessary.

Living in the Mansions and getting to know its bizarre albeit insightful inhabitants exposes Adah to many perspectives. She interacts with her fellow tenants, a lesson learned in the hospital maternity ward, and incorporates into her own being nuggets of their wisdom as well as their peculiar ways of dealing with the world. Adah's eyes are open to see life as it unfolds around her and in the end she profits from the experience. Her keen observations serve her well. She now comprehends what a wickedly alluring place the Mansions had been for her. Certainly, she had benefited from Carol's assistance and resources, after all Carol had been a good friend to her; but had some of her own resourcefulness and ingenuity remained dormant? Had she been lulled into some comatose state in which she was forced to rely on others for life's provisions? A crucial aspect of her *Bildungsprozess* is that she becomes aware of the complexities of the welfare system. Adah reflects on her situation: *"I have to be out of the ditch sometime, I have to learn to make my own decisions without running to Carol. I may or may not have any social officer any more. When I'm in need, I can always write to them. It does not pay to use somebody else as a means to an end"* (127).

The Mansions were to be torn down and rebuilt and most tenants left as soon as possible upon learning this. Those left are families behind in rent or those like Adah who are apprehensive about their future. It is after realizing that the Mansions were built over a cemetery that Adah realizes that her time to leave has come. She must delay no longer. She is determined to live no longer in the ditch—a literal and figurative graveyard from which an escape is nearly impossible. Whoopey reminds her about a certain Mr. Persial who has agreed to help them in locating new lodging and eventually Adah finds agreeable housing in the Matchbox flats near Regent's Park. Emecheta notes that "A week later, [Adah] moved out of the Mansions, away from the ditch, to face the world alone, without the cushioning comfort of Mrs. Cox, without the master-minding of Carol. It was time she became an individual" (127). Although life there is very different from the time she spent in the Mansions, Adah is "determined to enjoy her new surroundings" (128). She is at first a bit lonely in her new home; however, there is evidence that Adah soon adjusts to her new surroundings and independence. During a shopping trip, Adah runs into Whoopey who immediately notices changes in the *Bildungsheld*: "Have you come into a fortune, or did you win the pools?   My, you look different. You've changed a lot" (129). Adah's break from the chaos and filth of the Mansions allows her to arrive at a new, heightened sense of self. Adah has new resolve to make her existence count for something. More than ever she holds the promise to come into her own sense of being, become a writer, finish her education, continue to be an excellent mother, and always wait expectantly for arrival of future opportunity.

Emecheta's Autobiographical Novels

In the last two lines of the book, when Adah invites Whoopey to "come and see me sometimes," Whoopey responds: "Yes, I'd like to do that, but you're always out, aren't yer?" (135). The novel thus ends and readers are left to wonder what happens to Adah. While this might be evidence of her continued hard work raising her children, going to the market, and generally taking care of the odds and ends of life, an alternate interpretation, and one that is perhaps more plausible given Whoopey's previous remark concerning Adah's appearance, could be that she is out in the world creating her own individuated self. Adah no longer has the full welfare safety net beneath her and her family. Her children, for whom she has always taken full responsibility, are dependent upon a mother who can not only be there for them, but also exhibit strong qualities of selfhood. Emecheta's semi-autobiographical novels, *Second-Class Citizen* and *In the Ditch*, lend themselves clearly to female *Bildung* interpretation. While Adah remains committed to her family until an extreme breaking point and to the details of everyday life instead of overarching ideologies, she nonetheless clearly displays qualities of emerging selfhood and self-formation.

Christina Davis efficiently outlines character traits in Adah that create her subjectivity (17-18). They include determination, seen from early childhood by the great lengths to which she goes to get an education to the many small lies (for entrance examination, for contraception) she tells at various stages in her life; independence and rebelliousness, apparent when she chooses to raise her own children in London, something most African immigrants do not do; adaptability to ever-changing and difficult situations; assurance that she is doing the right thing when she leaves her husband; and finally a positive outlook as she prepares to leave the socially comfortable milieu of the Mansions. Adah's progress may be slow and methodical, or in Abel, Hirsch, and Langland's terms "more conflicted, less direct," yet she does grow, change and show promise for further self-affirmation.

The argument that Adah's growth and individuation, encouraged by her life in the West, are results of a personal deracination, a loss of a certain "Africanness" or native culture and tradition so vital to who she is must be addressed. Certainly there are critics who might admit that Adah undergoes a kind of *Bildungsprozess*, but the location, England and catalyst, Western opportunity for such education and change, makes her newly developing personhood less authentic than it might have been had she been able to stay in Nigeria. On the contrary, I would suggest that even before Adah met and married Francis and moved to London she demonstrated clear and unmistakable signs of *Bildung-*

sheld potential. Even in her native Nigeria, Adah was already an élite. Her education and motivation had already distinguished her among her African contemporaries. Another critical piece of evidence that indicates that Adah may not be as far removed from the culture and traditions of her native land as it seems is that she concentrates her artistic abilities on writing stories related to her African background. That *Second-Class Citizen* and *In the Ditch* are semi-autobiographical novels with Adah representing Emecheta attests to the fact that the self under development in question, be it Adah or Emecheta, has not compromised her native background in order to become another, less genuine self. Emecheta's writing brings her immense and surprising satisfaction. In an interview with Davidson and Marie Umeh, Emecheta claims that *Second-Class Citizen* "established [her] as an independent writer and made [her] financially secure" (24). The acts of writing and telling, for Emecheta as well as her alter ego Adah, help to establish a confident self able to see more and get more out of life than if these avenues of self-expression had not been explored. Without question, Adah and Emecheta are "as cunning as a serpent but as harmless as a dove," attributes that bode well as they seek authentic and balanced selfhood in the face of the complexities of colonial and patriarchal forces.

Note

1 In 1965 Ghanian president Nkrumah coined the term neo-colonialism in *Neo-Colonialism: The Last Stage of Imperialism*. He felt that ex-colonial and newly emergent powers as well as the élite or *comprador* class of native leaders continued to perpetuate imperialistic conditions through control of world markets, marginalization of critical contributions by developing peoples, and by failure to represent constituents in matters crucial to balanced development of individual countries in a post-independence context.

Chapter 4

The "Lightening of Various Darknesses": Tambu's Tortuous Path to Development in Tsitsi Dangarembga's *Nervous Conditions*

> *"I feel many things these days, much more than I was able to feel in the days when I was young. . ., and there are reasons for this more than the mere consequence of age . . . my story is not after all about death, but about my escape"* Tambu, narrator and *Bildungsheld* of Dangarembga's *Nervous Conditions*

In the seventeen years since Zimbabwean author Tsitsi Dangarembga's only novel, her semi-autobiographical *Nervous Conditions*, first appeared it has acquired high praise, generated insightful critical commentary and, along with other novels by African women before and after it (Bâ, Nwapa, Emecheta, Beyala, Aidoo to name a few), helped to elucidate the realities and complexities of race, class, and gender in colonial and post-colonial spaces. Dangarembga's native Zimbabwe has a long history which connects the country directly to European history as far back as the early 1500s. Portuguese explorers arrived in present day Zimbabwe in the first part of the sixteenth century and cut off trade and began wars that severely weakened the country for decades. The Portuguese were forced to leave around 1690, but the British began mining gold there in 1888. Many skirmishes ensued and when the British defeated the Ndebele people in 1893, immigration of white Europeans was fully underway. Several pieces of British legislation were passed; one kept Africans from owning any of the more fertile farming lands while another banned them from practicing trades or professions. Rhodesia, as Zimbabwe was first called, under the leadership of Prime Minister Ian Smith, called for independence in 1963, but their independence was not gained until 1965. The name of the country was later changed to Zimbabwe. Dangarembga now writes and studies in Europe but remains well connected to her Zimbabwean culture and traditions.

The first novel by a black Zimbabwean female to reach readers' hands would not have done so if not for the British run Women's Press since Dangarembga's first attempts to publish her novel in her native country failed. In an interview with Jane Wilkinson, Dangarembga states that at the time the manuscript was turned down she remembers wondering if "this decision from [the Zimbabwean] publishing house really reflected the fact that [she] could not write, or did it reflect perhaps the fact that [she] was writing about things that they were not ready to read about" (197). Pauline Ada Uwakweh reminds us that "patriarchal subordination of the female is reflected in the male domination of the literary arena" as well, which likely accounts for the initial rejection of Dangarembga's text for publication and undoubtedly is responsible for so many skewed and unrealistic representations of females in African literature by males ("Debunking Patriarchy . . . " 75). Uwakweh adds "the autobiographical mode adopted by Dangarembga as a literary strategy marks her attainment of voice in the Zimbabwean male-dominated literary arena" ("Debunking Patriarchy . . . " 75). Dangarembga's novel, characterized by its persistent interrogation of the roles of male characters vis à vis female characters and by association the overarching African and Western patriarchal structures in general and its insistence on varied yet linked "mechanisms of oppression" (race, class, culture and gender), has been classified as a *transformative* feminist text by Susan Arndt (85). Similarly, the complexity of the novel's treatment of these "mechanisms of oppression" has prompted M. Keith Booker to claim that "one of the most important achievements of *Nervous Conditions* is its demonstration of the complicity between colonialism and patriarchy, which function not merely as simultaneous forms of parallel oppression, but as inseparable parts of the same phenomenon" (199). *Nervous Conditions* has been received as a well-written text that strives to be honest, brutally honest at times, as it recounts "[Tambu's] escape and Lucia's; about [Tambu's] mother's and Maiguru's entrapment; and about Nyasha's rebellion . . . [which] may not in the end have been successful" (Dangarembga 1). While it is undoubtedly the story of the effects of colonialism and patriarchy, it is also very much the story of varying degrees of personal development for five women. Specifically, *Nervous Conditions* functions as a modern African *Bildungsroman* as it portrays the conflicted path and ultimate enlightenment and escape of the young Tambu.

While one of the five women and the narrator of the story, Tambu, appears to be more successful in her quest for socialization and a new found identity than the other four, M. Keith Booker suggests that the impact of the story is far greater than that singular character's experience (190). He continues:

> the changes that Tambudzai [Tambu] undergoes in the course of her education and maturation clearly parallel historical changes that were underway in colonial Zimbabwe (then called Rhodesia). Thus the personal experiences of the protagonist are linked with public events in her society in ways that make her an emblem of her society and also serve as a reminder that individuals always develop within specific historical contexts. (Booker 190)

Tambu becomes a kind of "individual character in postcolonial fiction whose experience embodies that of an entire nation as it emerges from colonialism"— Fredric Jameson's "national allegory" or Lukács's "typical" character[1] (Booker 190). Indeed many African literary characters manifest in their personal existences various social, historical or cultural phenomena.

Nervous Conditions has been referred to as either a *Bildungsroman* or a novel of development by Mary Jane Androne, Flora Veit-Wild, Pauline Ada Uwakweh, Florence Stratton and others. Thus, its generic status has been well established. It is sometimes the case with novels that depict growth, maturation, and formation that literary critics invoke the term *Bildungsroman* rather nonchalantly as they head in divergent directions to examine related yet varying thematics. More often than not, such appellation does not compromise the critique. However, we would all do well, this writer included, to remember Jeffrey Sammons's words of caution—"the farther away one gets from [the] roots [of the origins of the term *Bildung* or *Bildungsroman*], the more careful one should be about defining the term and justifying its utility" (41-2). While the defining and justifying took place in Chapter One of this book, the objective then of this chapter involves a synthesis of previous critical examinations of the work in terms of genre classification not only to arrive at a unified perspective, but also to collect evidence toward a summation of Dangarembga's contributions to the African *Bildungsroman* in relationship to the other African female writers considered in this book.

Nervous Conditions chronicles the story of the social, intellectual, esthetic and psychological development of a central protagonist, Tambudzai (Tambu) Sigauke, as she interacts with members of her extended family, most notably her mother, two aunts, and her cousin. Tambu, much like Emecheta's young Adah, realizes quickly that her education is not as much of a priority as that of her brother, Nhamo. Nhamo, the only male child in the family, has been given the singular opportunity of studying at the mission school, only twenty miles and an hour's drive from the homestead but much farther ideologically and materially,

where his English educated uncle Babamukuru is headmaster and local education guru. Tambu's thoughts on her brother and his fortuity are unmistakable. In
what amounts to a balanced and effective mixture of first-person and third-
person omniscient points of view, Dangarembga transfers her authorial preroga-
tives to Tambu, allowing her to "author" or narrate her story thus giving her a
voice of her own. Given the discussion of autobiography in Chapter Two, this is
also one of the first indications in this novel that Tambu is a *Bildungsheld* and
her story a *Bildungsroman.* "The narrator," suggests Uwakweh, "occupies an
interpretive position, a perspective that is necessary for our appreciation of the
new insights she acquires about her experience as a female in a patriarchal and
colonial society" ("Debunking Patriarchy . . . " 75). These insights also clearly
recount multifarious growth as an individual.

In Chapter One of the novel Tambu is not short on expressions of hatred
and resentment for Nhamo. In the first paragraph, Tambu exclaims that she "was
not sorry when her brother died" and that she is not "apologising for [her] cal-
lousness, . . . for [her] lack of feeling" (1). We quickly learn the reason for such
a shocking opening remark. It is the death of Nhamo that opens a spot for her at
the mission school. Babamukuru had earlier revealed his master plan in a family
meeting that each branch of his family tree have at least one educated person to
build that extension of the family up socially, intellectually, and ultimately financially. When Nhamo dies, Tambu becomes her family's salvation. Even
though she is aware of her status as second choice, prospects of the new adventure certainly excite Tambu; she "was triumphant. Babamukuru had approved of
[her] direction. [She] was vindicated!" (57). Yet, Tambu's feelings of inequity
are ever present:

> The needs and sensibilities of the women in my family were not con-
> sidered a priority, or even legitimate. That was why I was in Standard
> Three in the year that Nhamo died, instead of in Standard Five, as I
> should have been by that age. In those days I felt the injustice of my
> situation every time I thought about it, which I could not help but do
> often since children are always talking about their age. Thinking
> about it, feeling the injustice of it, this is how I came to dislike my
> brother, and not only my brother: my father, my mother—in fact eve-
> rybody. (12)

For Tambu, it is also Nhamo's snobbery and the haughty attitude he acquires
after he leaves home, his refusal to carry his own luggage when he arrives at the
compound from school, and his cruelty in stealing the mealies she had grown to
pay for her initial education opportunities locally, that fuel her bitterness.

The reader counts it a privilege to have the advantage of a mature narrator
in Tambu who is able to put the pieces of the puzzle back together as she relates
the events of her development from childhood forward. Several times in the
story we are informed that Tambu has come to such and such realization later in
life, that she can assert this or that because of what she now knows. One such
instance concerns her brother. Tambu notes:

> I was quite sure at the time that Nhamo knew as well as I did that the things he had said were not reasonable, but in the years that have passed since then I have met so many men who consider themselves responsible adults and therefore ought to know better, who still subscribe to the fundamental principles of my brother's budding elitism, that to be fair to him I must conclude that he was sincere in his bigotry. (49)

This realization, which comes after years of growth, development, education and observation, exposes the serious effects of colonialism for these African characters. "Dangarembga . . . ," writes Uwakweh, "questions the exploitative nature of imperialism, the value of Western education, and warns against the danger of cultural alienation that it poses to the African" ("Debunking Patriarchy . . . " 77). It appears that Tambu, later in life, comprehends the causes of her brother's snooty behavior and rude actions; she does in fact admit: "I feel many things these days, much more than I was able to feel in the days when my brother died, and there are reasons for this more than the mere consequence of age" (1). Tambu's insights, gained through personal development and *Bildung*, prove critical to Dangarembga's message concerning colonialism, patriarchy and possibilities of expansion.

We are told that Nhamo falls prey to "Englishness" and while his death is essentially shrouded in mystery, the pressures inherent in his adoption of Western ways coupled with his inheritance of African patriarchal ways seemingly take his life. While Nhamo is the only character to die from such an "affliction," he is certainly not the only character to become sick and suffer from various nervous conditions. Such sickness reoccurs in Tambu's mother Mainini, in Maiguru, and especially in Nyasha throughout the novel, and while the disease of "Englishness," of patriarchy and colonialism affect Tambu, she manages to transcend or escape its debilitating grasp. Interestingly, Dangarembga states that she chose the title for her first novel after it had been written and when she was introduced by a friend to Frantz Fanon's *Les damnés de la terre*, 1961 (*The Wretched of the Earth*). It is in Jean-Paul Sartre's preface to Fanon's theoretical work that the phrase "The condition of native is a nervous condition" appears. It leapt out to her and became not only source material for her title but an epigraph to the novel as well appearing as the whole sentence does on the flyleaf. Charles Sugnet notes the "amazing areas of overlap (and important areas of difference) between Fanon's theory and Dangrembga's novel, especially with regard to colonial psychology and the manifestation of resistance through physical symptoms" (35). And Dangarembga most likely was intrigued by the slight double meaning of the term nervous condition—"nervous in the ordinary sense of anxious, uneasy, or worried, but also in the formal medical or psychiatric sense of 'so and so suffers from a nervous condition'"—when considered in connection with her narrative (Sugnet 35). Pluralizing Sartre's "diagnosis" and affixing it to her cover and title page, Dangarembga creates an apt title replete with rich layers of meaning and theoretical moorings to boot.

The Other Women and Their Men

"but the story I have told here, is my own story, the story of four
women whom I loved, and our men, this story is how it all began."
Tambu, *Nervous Conditions*

Before discussing Tambu's *Bildungsprozess* in great detail, it is necessary
to examine in closer detail the nervous conditions alluded to earlier in several of
the other characters. Such analyses serve to demonstrate the extreme nature of
anguish the women characters undergo in this text. They also set up the contrast
between the various ways in which four of them handle their difficult circumstances and how Tambu ultimately enlightens her darkness. Tambu acknowledges herself that, "this story [the story of the five women and their men] is how
it all began" (Dangarembga 204). Even though both of Tambu's parents are
somewhat skeptical about educating their children outside the local village, it is
Mainini who, throughout the course of the novel, speaks out to express her concerns over Western influence through schooling and association with those who
have been to England. Tambu's father, Jeremiah, is a sad case, indeed, and another representation of the atrocities than can be visited on African males under
colonialism. Repeatedly, critics such as Margaret Strobel point to the emasculat-
ing powers of Westernization on African males and novelists chronicle the same
phenomenon in their works[2]. Jeremiah remains a victim of psychological emasculation primarily because of perceived inferiority to his "been-to" brother Babamukuru, but also because of the encroaching influence of colonizers upon the
village that Tambu recounts at the beginning of the text. Because of his lack of
vision and conviction and the ease with which he can be swayed and convinced
on matters, Jeremiah accepts freely and without question or reflection Babamukuru's offer to educate first Nhamo and later Tambu at the heavily European
influenced mission school. On the other hand, Mainini has always been wary of
the things to which Nhamo was being exposed at the mission. When Nhamo
returns home for vacation she notices not only the natural changes in his physical appearance, but his fluent use of English and the loss of his native Shona.
Dangarembga records this mother's anxiety thus: "My mother was alarmed. She
knew that the mission was a Christian place. Nevertheless she maintained that
the people there were ordinary people. She thought someone on the mission was
bewitching her son and was all for making an appointment with the medium. . . .
She did want him to be educated, . . . but even more, she wanted to talk to him"
(53). Much more dramatic is her reaction to the news regarding Nhamo's death.
Mainini undergoes a complete breakdown—

> Without warning my mother keened shrilly through the dark silence.
> 'Go back!' she wailed. 'Go back! Why do you come all this way to
> tell me what I already know!' She collapsed on to the car bonnet,
> slipped to the ground, picked herself up and collapsed again. . . .
> First you took his tongue so that he could not speak to me and now

you have taken everything, taken everything for good. . . . You be-
witched him and now he is dead. . . . You [Babamukuru and Mai-
guru] and your education have killed my son. This time when she fell
to the ground she did not pick herself up, but rolled there, tearing her
hair and her clothes and grinding sand between her teeth. (54)

Mainini's condition never again leaves her throughout the novel. In fact, on
learning that her daughter would now go to study at the mission, her symptoms
intensify—"she ate hardly anything, not for lack of trying, and when she was
able to swallow something it lay heavy in her stomach. By the time [Tambu] left
she was so haggard and gaunt she could hardly walk to the fields, let alone work
in them" (57). Later, when Mainini learns that Tambu will go to the convent
school she stops taking care of herself completely—"[s]he ate less and less and
did less and less, until within days she could neither eat nor do anything, not
even change the dress she wore" (184). In addition, her carelessness with feeding her newborn results in his contraction of diarrhea. Clearly, the encroachment
of an elaborate web of colonial and patriarchal structures triggers in Mainini a
detrimental reaction that casts her into darkness and essentially causes her nervous breakdown. Being cared for by her younger sister, Lucia, and getting back to
the cleansing waters of the Nyamarira, the local river, thus receiving what
Tambu calls "a sort of shock treatment," help assuage Mainini's condition. Instead of focusing on all the misfortunes that the outside power structures had
presumably caused her and her family; she, through a dip in the river and Lucia's "therapy," is refocused through healing qualities of native elements and
reconnection with family.

As is clear, Mainini's nervous condition is manifested outwardly through
physical affliction and abnormal behavior; however, that of Maiguru largely
remains undisclosed. After all, Maiguru in appearance seems whole and healthy.
She has received an education in South Africa and even a Master's Degree in
England and not only works as a teacher at the mission school but also takes
care of her husband, her children and is certain that they are well fed and happy.
Sugnet calls her "the unhappy 'Superwoman'" and notes that she is exemplary
in terms of self-growth and individuation to a certain degree (42). The Westernization she has undergone by receiving an English education does not ultimately
lead to all the freedoms she might have hoped for and cannot be the sole and
simple path to liberation or formation for Tambu (Sugnet 42). Tambu learns, not
long after her arrival at the mission, that although Maiguru is just as educated as
her husband Babamukuru, she never directly receives payment for her teaching
duties at the school. Her pay goes straight to her husband. Although Dangarembga, through Tambu, alludes to her inner patience and generosity, readers are
ultimately made aware of Maiguru's self-denial and general acquiescence.
Khani Begum reminds us that "It is not till after Tambu has lived in Maiguru's
house for some time that she comes to realize that even Maiguru, an educated
and employable modern woman, is being crushed by the weight of womanhood
and that her mother's warning holds true for all black women" (24). This weight

gets so burdensome that at one point Maiguru leaves her husband and household for a few days and stays with her brother. Physical manifestations are never really a part of Maiguru's suffering; however, she does find it necessary to remove herself at least temporarily from her environment, a praiseworthy move according to her daughter Nyasha.

Maiguru grows tired of following Babamukuru's orders about how to take care of their extended family, provide a "proper" wedding for his brother and sister-in-law, Tambu's parents, and offer money and lodging to anyone expressing the slightest need. She is tired of "being nothing in a home [she is] working [herself] sick to support" (172). Maiguru admits "his nerves were bad. His nerves were bad because he was so busy" (102). It is difficult for Babamukuru to be a representative of the West in his home country all the while insuring that the natives do the right things and make the most of their lives, thus he winds up overworked and always on edge with those who love him most. Nevertheless, this is Maiguru's daily environment and although "[her] education and employment allow her to question male dominance, she does not possess the means to do anything about it" (Begum 25). The five days away from the household seemingly refresh Maiguru since she returns with smiles and a pleasant disposition. It appears that her time outside Babamukuru's "position of economic power that reinforces his authority as head of the family" allowed for a purging of repressed abilities, emotions, and possibilities (Booker 197-98).

Undoubtedly the character in the novel that suffers most due to the domineering web of colonial and patriarchal pressures is Nyasha. Like Dangarembga, Nyasha is educated for several years in England when her parents take up study for Master's Degrees there (Wilkinson 188). When the family returns to Rhodesia (Zimbabwe), she is a changed individual. First cousin Tambu "[misses] the bold, ebullient companion [she] had had who had gone to England but had not returned from there" (51). Nyasha appears sickly and silent and refuses to socialize, to play games and to reconnect with her extended family. She is pushed into the dark corners of extended family interactions. She has forgotten how to speak Shona further alienating her from her native culture and traditions. Yet readers soon become aware that Nyasha's assessment of her predicament and the overall effects on her family because of time spent in the West are frighteningly sound. Nyasha has no friends in school and her status as loner allows her to reflect deeply on her circumstances. She is intelligent and full of questions about history and international politics, but she is also practical and humorous on occasion as well. She offers tampons as Tambu learns to negotiate her first menstrual cycle. She is aware of the latest in style and fashion and that sleek and svelte is better than curvaceous and plump. She smokes, enjoys staying out late with boys and reads D. H. Lawrence's *Lady Chatterley's Lover*. After some time together, Tambu offers telling assessments of her cousin:

> That cousin of mine! Shocking and funny; disrespectful and irre-
> pressible. I was no longer wary now that I knew who she was. I
> thought she was wise too, although I was not sure why. I admired her

abundance of spirit even though I could not see where it was directed: Nyasha had everything, should have been placid and content. My cousin was perplexing. She was not something you could dissect with reason . . . Nyasha . . . was persistently seeing and drawing attention to things you would rather not talk about; shredding to bits with her sharp wit the things she thought we could do without, even if everybody else thought they were important. People like me thought she was odd and rather superior in intangible ways. Peripheral adults like her teachers thought she was a genius and encouraged this aspect of her. (96-7)

Until Tambu's time at the convent school, the two remain the closest of friends and without a doubt, Nyasha positively influences Tambu's *Bildungsprozess*.

On several occasions, Nyasha offers perceptive explanations for why she and her family are in the condition they are in. They all amount to the inescapable influence Western education had on their lives while they lived in England. Nyasha especially finds it difficult to reconnect with her African roots after being away. Accusingly, Nyasha speaks:

'They've done it to me.' . . . 'Really they have.' . . . 'It's not their fault. They did it to them too. You know they did,' she whispered. 'To both of them [her parents], but especially to him [her father].' . . . 'Why do they do it, Tambu,' she hissed bitterly, her face contorting with rage, 'to me and to you and to him? Do you see what they've done? They've taken us away. . . . They've deprived you of you, him of him, ourselves of each other. We're grovelling. . . . She began to rock, her body quivering tensely. . . . 'I won't grovel, I won't die,' she raged and crouched like a cat ready to spring. (200)

Afterward, Nyasha breaks down and rips the pages from her history book calling its contents lies.

Nyasha also suffers from what Dangarembga terms anorexia and Lindsay P. Aegerter writes that Nyasha "embodies the 'nervous conditions' Fanon ascribes to all colonized subjects" (237). Aegerter also asserts that Nyasha seeks to reconnect with her original identity and that her growing relationship with Tambu allows this to begin to take place (237-38). When Tambu leaves the mission late in the novel to enroll at the Sacred Heart School, however, "Nyasha is stripped of the strength—the healing laughter—that accompanies camaraderie. She quickly succumbs to the 'nervous conditions' her friendship with Tambudzai had deferred" (Aegerter 237). She ends up so sickly that her body can hardly function. Many critics have described Nyasha's reaction as a literal embodiment of her pitiable circumstances. She would sit at the dinner table and eat because her parents insisted and then she would rush off to the toilet, gag herself with her toothbrush thus causing her body eventually to appear "grotesquely unhealthy from the vital juices she flushed down the toilet" (199). Likewise, she is so obsessed with her academic pursuits that she studies long hours in order to be able to perform well on tests.

Like Mainini and to a much lesser extent Maiguru, Nyasha finds it difficult to lay claim to her own selfhood. Detached from her African individuality because of her family's experience in England, she fights to break free from the colonial capitalism and patriarchal forces that command their lives. Her life presents one irony after another: her family has money to enjoy a bounty of food, yet she either refuses it or when forced to eat, makes herself vomit it later in the toilet; she has enjoyed advantage beyond that of many others, yet she cannot find day to day happiness. At the end of the novel, after Nyasha's warning that she too is at risk, Tambu wonders "if Nyasha who had everything could not make it, where could I expect to go? . . . Nyasha's progress was still in the balance, and so, as a result, was [Tambu's]" (202). Even though Tambu becomes entangled in the forces of colonization and experiences patriarchal oppression during her quest for education and *Bildung*, she manages to transcend their clutches unlike the four other women in her story. Tambu's *Bildungsprozess* allows her to pursue knowledge and larger life experiences while at the same time remaining grounded in her African culture and traditions.

Tambu's Path Out of Darkness

> *"Thus began the period of my reincarnation. . . . I expected this era to be significantly profound and broadening in terms of adding wisdom to my nature, clarity to my vision. . . . It was a centripetal time, with me at the centre, everything was gravitating towards me. It was a time of sublimation with me as the sublimate."*   Tambu, *Nervous Conditions*

Tambu's story is clearly a modern African *Bildung* story despite the fact that life is never easy in any sense for the young girl. Tambu's childhood is similar in many ways to Adah's childhood in Emecheta's novels. Both girls desire education early on and both face the realities and hardships of a native culture which privileges sons over daughters. Whereas Adah shows ingenuity early on by sneaking off to school with a make-shift slate on which to write, Tambu gets to attend school when and if the crops yield, but is two Standards behind where she should be considering her age. Adah insures the continuance of her education by working hard for scholarships and because someone convinced her mother, at the death of her father, that the more education Adah had, the more money she would fetch at her marriage. The assurance and acceleration of Tambu's education occurs at the death of her brother an event which triggers the opening sentence of the novel: "I was not sorry when my brother died" (1). As first person narrator who is now an adult, Tambu profits from the ability to look into her past and see that it is Nhamo's death that leads to her journey down the path of development.

Tambu is the second child of Jeremiah and Mainini Sigauke who live on the rural homestead once belonging to Jeremiah's side of the family. Even though their immediate family is not well off, it is neither poor; yet Jeremiah's brother Babamukuru, who has studied for a Master's Degree in England, sees Jeremiah's branch of the family as the neediest of the four branches. In a position to act on his assessment, Babamukuru, headmaster at the mission school twenty miles from the homestead, offers to have first Nhamo and then Tambu live with his family and study at the school. The opportunity ruins Nhamo in the eyes of his immediate family, as he becomes self-centered and snobbish during his days at the school. After his life mysteriously comes to an early end, the school becomes the open door to Tambu's path to self-affirmation and subjectivity.

If Emecheta's Adah sees the United Kingdom as the Kingdom of Heaven, then for Tambu, in Dangarembga's *Nervous Conditions*, Babamukuru is God. And just as Adah's viewpoint is a product of her naïveté, Tambu's early perspective of her uncle fails to reveal his shortcomings and by association the greater flaws within colonialism and the difficulties for women in patriarchal societies. Booker admits that "Tambudzai is greatly intimidated by her domineering uncle, partially for the simple reason that he is in a position of patriarchal authority, but also because of the aura of his European education" (193). Yet, he also fascinates her. Tambu is drawn to her uncle because he holds the keys to her education and ultimately her future. His family lives the modern life with attendant luxuries including an inside toilet, nice furnishings, and a servant named Anna. The bitterness she has felt because of ongoing inequality of opportunities, specifically in education, for males and females becomes less of an issue when it appears that she too will be able to study at the mission and be exposed to life outside the homestead. Rahul K. Gairola notes that "For Tambu, Westernization is a necessity, even after she witnesses the mental demise of Nyasha and, early in the novel, is disgusted by the fact that Nhamo has forgotten Shona" (par. 11). Tambu is determined to take advantage of all that is available to her—her assessment of the day she departs the homestead reveals her early expectations:

> What I experienced that day was a short cut, a rerouting of everything I had ever defined as me into fast lanes that would speedily lead me to my destination. My horizons were saturated with me, my leaving, my going. There was no room for what I left behind. . . . At Babamukuru's I would have the leisure, be encouraged to consider questions that had to do with survival of the spirit, the creation of consciousness, rather than mere sustenance of the body. (58-9)

Life has seemingly turned around for Tambu. Her *Bildung* path is becoming more and more clear.

After arriving at the mission school, Tambu soaks up her new surroundings like a sponge. It is in these surroundings that, for the first time in her life, she begins to experience the esthetics of life, a necessary first step on her path toward self-expansion. She is amazed at what she sees and her mind races as she wonders about this or that building, about where she might sleep, and about flowers that "had been planted for joy" (64). While Tambu revels in seeing Babamukuru's mansion and the various school buildings herself, even though she still recalls her brother's boastful descriptions, it is the realization that people put plants in the ground simply to be enjoyed that makes a lasting impression. In her experience on the homestead, things were planted for the utilitarian purposes of food and for income and her grandmother, "inexorable cultivator of land, sower of seeds and reaper of rich harvests until . . . her very last moment," had "consolidated it in [Tambu] as a desirable habit" (17). The mealies Tambu plants not long before her arrival at the mission grow to provide money for school and now, as if she is from a different world, she sees "a blaze of canna lilies burning scarlet and amber" (64). She is grateful for her new experiences and for her uncle's generosity for now she too could conceive of cultivating "for merrier reasons than the chore of keeping breath in the body. . . . [She] would ask Maiguru for some bulbs and plant a bed of those gay lilies on the homestead. . . . Bright and cheery, they had been planted for joy. What a strange idea that was. It was a liberation, the first of many that followed from [her] transition to the mission" (64). The *Bildungsheld* gains exposure to and experience with the esthetic side of living; certainly this realization is the first of many for Tambu as she prepares to enter her uncle's mansion.

Although the adolescent Tambu is astonished at what she finds in the headmaster's mansion, the adult Tambu as narrator now realizes how not everything really matched and how the kitchen window was missing a pane. Young Tambu marvels at the delicate china, the eight-person dining room table and the living room furnishings. Tambu observes:

> If I was daunted by Maiguru's dainty porcelain cups, the living-
> room . . . would have finished me off had I not been inoculated by the
> gradient [of seeing the less striking rooms first]. . . . This increase in
> comfort from kitchen to living-room was a common feature of all the
> teachers' houses at the mission. It had more to do with means and
> priorities than taste. Babamukuru's taste was excellent, so that where
> he could afford to indulge it, the results were striking. The opulence
> of his living-room was very strong stuff, overwhelming to someone
> who had first crawled and then toddled and finally walked over dung
> floors. (69)

Immediately Tambu is hit by the reality of her reason for being there. She must prevent such comfortable surroundings from lulling her away from her educational objectives. She does not want to be the victim of opulence she supposes Nhamo was. Her strategy, when the "thinking strategy" does not work, is to remain "as aloof and unimpressed as possible" (69-70). Soon however, the newness of her surrounding is gone and Tambu realizes that even in a house so seemingly dirt free, a thin layer of dust constantly covers every surface due to unusually heavy bus traffic traversing the mission's dirt streets. While Tambu's initial impressions with life at the mission, the lilies, the mansion and its contents, jump start her *Bildungsprozess*, it is her interactions with people, notably other females and books, that have the greatest effect on her.

Lindsay P. Aegerter states that the women in Dangarembga's novel "redefine their roles as 'women' and as 'African' within a womanist epistemology that recognizes allegiance to traditional heritage *and* to women's emancipation" (231). Although this distinction between Western feminism and African feminism has already been discussed elsewhere in this book, it is important here to note Aegerter's attempts to characterize further the communal aspects responsible for allowing women to experience freedom while clinging to tradition. She privileges Bakhtinian dialogue (or dialogics) and community exchanges between African women and cites Mae Gwendolyn Henderson who finds African women's writing interlocutory or dialogical in nature. Henderson envisages dialogues between two or more individuals or as interior conversations taking place in a single individual (Aegerter 232). Undoubtedly, it is Tambu's interactions with her family members that help her locate her own subjectivity.

The person with whom Tambu maintains consistent communication is her first cousin Nyasha. Although their relationship is a bit awkward at the beginning of the narrative because Nyasha has just returned from an extended stay in England and she behaves very differently, Tambu, strangely enough, is later drawn to her. From the way she dresses and the way she acts the first day they see each other again after the long separation, Tambu knows that Nyasha has indeed been to England. Tambu is astonished that Nyasha has forgotten the native language of Shona. She is dismayed that on that first night back at the homestead her cousins refused to take part in the dancing and festivities as they once had before their stay in England:

> Chido [Nyasha's brother] declined [to dance] politely. . . . Nyahsa clicked her tongue scornfully and switched herself off. It was very abrupt the way she did it. . . . I [Tambu] went outside trying very hard not to let the episode spoil the rest of the evening. It was difficult though. I had been looking forward to having my cousins back so that things would be fun and friendly and warm as they had been in the old days, but it was not happening that way. (43)

Things do not get much better for a while, yet Tambu remains intrigued in a sense by her cousin whose precociousness makes everyone a bit uneasy. Tambu confesses: "Everytime my relatives came from the mission I stayed near Nyasha, and watched her. In this way I saw her observing us all. . . . She was silent and watchful, observing us all with that complex expression of hers . . . with an intensity that made me uncomfortable" (52). Later when Tambu is chosen to study at the mission it does not take long for the two girls to grow close and share their thoughts and feelings.

As Tambu engages in her studies at the mission, she moves in some senses farther and farther away from the person she was on the homestead. Her courses, the books to which she is exposed and the people she meets contribute to her

Bildungsprozess. Finally her wish "to find another self, a clean, well-groomed, genteel self who could not have been bred, could not have survived on the homestead" slowly materializes (58-9). Sally McWilliams suggests however that while the interactions between Tambu and Nyasha contribute to this process, they also complicate it:

> Tambu's self-conscious search for an identity reveals the complexities of the "I" position. She sees herself growing insipid and tentative at the mission school; her "concrete and categorical" self from her younger days is partially eclipsed as she attempts to understand the enigma that is her cousin Nyasha. (75)

> For Tambu, Nyasha is that small part of herself which is adventurous and explorative; everything about Nyasha spoke of alternatives that could wreck Tambu's linear plans for her education and for a clear-cut, wholly unambiguous sense of identity. (104-05)

Tambu learns that the path to a "clean, well-groomed, genteel self" is a tortuous one indeed. Nyahsa seems to have the education, sophistication, and individual sense of identity that Tambu so desperately wants; however, for Nyasha, these things have come at a cost.

Nyasha's exposure to Western ways has made her a highly analytical, non-conforming individual who constantly and uncompromisingly calls received and accepted ideas and notions into question. "Through much of the text," writes Booker, "Tambudzai is so dazzled by the material opportunities offered by colonial culture that she is unable to understand the potential disadvantages of colonialism. Growing up in England, Nyasha is less dazzled . . . and more able to mount a critique of colonialism" (194). Nyasha is able to see beyond the black and white of issues—her perspective implies "shades and textures within the same colour" (Dangarembga 164). She openly disapproves of her mother's self-determined lowered status vis à vis her father even though they have the same level of education, she believes her father is a simple puppet of the colonizers, "a good boy, a good munt. A bloody good kaffir," who thinks in and promotes an oversimplified binary take on life and she seems to see through the overall illusion of the colonial project (200). Tambu shows concern as Nyasha's sense of coherent selfhood unravels, as her cousin's relationship with her parents is strained and as she suffers physically with anorexia. But Tambu focuses all the more on making the most of her own new experiences. According to McWilliams:

> Tambu's struggle for self-identity evolves into an awareness of her heteroglot complexity. She comes to sense that her identity is a composite of shifting selves; she is not only obedient, hard-working, self-abnegating, she is also adventurous, rebellious, strong-willed in her dialogically enervated positions as daughter, cousin, niece, schoolgirl, confidante and self. (105)

Tambu successfully balances her new life and her new roles with the way her life used to be on the homestead. She acclimates almost without incident as she discovers her new identity.

Even though the adult Tambu is later able to see their individual imperfections, people naturally play a large role in Tambu's early development. Babamukuru is the embodiment of intellect and decisive leadership, Maiguru is the dutiful, albeit educated wife, and Nyasha is the alter ego whose perceptions of the surrounding world challenge Tambu to see differently. Books too play a critical role in Tambu's formation. At multiple points in the story, she mentions their influence. In fact, in one such instance, Tambu, not unlike Zilia in de Graffigny's *Lettre d'une peruvienne*, grants that most of the knowledge she garners at the mission is derived from reading. Tambu reflects upon "Nyasha's various and extensive library" (93) and she recalls:

> I read everything from Enid Blyton to the Brontë sisters, and responded to them all. Plunging into these books I knew I was being educated and I was filled with gratitude to the authors for introducing me to places where reason and inclination were not at odds. It was a centripetal time, with me at the centre, everything was gravitating toward me. It was a time of sublimation with me as the sublimate. (93)

Tambu's literary encounters advance her ever-evolving selfhood and take their places beside the vast and priceless repertoire of stories told to her in the fields as a child by her grandmother. Sugnet writes: "For both Tambu and Nyasha, identity will be a shifting third term, composed and recomposed from an overlay of culturally various sources[3]: Shona and language ritual, trashy romance novels, stories told by grandmother, *Lady Chatterley's Lover*, . . . Alcott's *Little Women*, histories of Africa's colonization, novels by the Brontës, etc." (42). Tambu seems to deal more successfully with her changing identities and situations while Nyasha is compelled to confront any sort of injustice—she perceives her life is full of them. Carola Torti, Karin Kilb and Mark Stein contend that "[t]he subtler contradictions discerned by and harmful to Nyasha are overlooked by Tambu" (252). Thus Nyasha's analytical abilities develop into her worst enemy. Tambu's "strategy of staving off dangerous thoughts—thoughts that question her own situation—serves as a means of survival. 'I thought I was wise to be preserving my energy, unlike my cousin, who was burning herself out' (116)" (Torti, Kilb, and Stein 252). The fact that Tambu reaches a sense of self is made evident in the various interjections the adult narrator of "her" story is capable of making as she looks back at the ways her perceptions have changed from her time on the homestead, through her studies at the mission and ultimately at Sacred Heart.

Elleke Boehmer postulates that since the 1970s women of color around the world have sought to distinguish their project from that of Western feminism, and "Literature . . . was a powerful medium through which self-definition was sought. [For] a woman to tell her own story was to call into being an image of autonomous selfhood" (225). Dangarembga acknowledges that *Nervous Conditions* is in fact an autobiographical text with Nyasha and Tambu, each in her own way, representing aspects of the author's actual life. Albeit fiction, the fact that Tambu tells the story of her life demonstrates that she, like Dangarembga, has come the closest among the women she knows best to arriving at authentic individuation and is willing to share her story with readers. Sharing one's own story is not only a sign of confidence in the individual one has become, it is also a means, according to Henderson as we have seen, to the "development of black feminist consciousnesses" through communal dialogue and personal reflection and pronouncement (Aegerter 232). As Nyasha breaks down, Tambu, in what amounts to both a communal and reflective effort, recounts. How is it, many have asked, that Tambu is more successful than any one else in the novel, even those who have seemingly had more opportunities than she has had? How does she claim subjectivity when so many others, women and men alike, in the novel fail?

Without a doubt hard work figures prominently in Tambu's process of individuation. She is focussed and determined to make something of her life. Lack of sorrow at her brother's death and her ingenuity early on in selling green mealies for tuition money attest to her drive. In addition, the example of hard work modeled by both her mother and grandmother, not in libraries but in agricultural fields, resonates with Tambu throughout her academic studies. She does not take her opportunities lightly and "[invests] a lot of robust energy in approximating to [her] idea of a young woman in the world" (93). Hard work, according to Juliana Makuchi Nfah-Abbenyi, "could also serve as a driving force, as a space within which other valuable experiences and roles can infuse themselves" (66). For the young Tambu, stories emanating from and chronicling the details of her native traditions become crucial to her successes on the pathway to development.

Not only does her grandmother's example of hard work influence her, but her grandmother's stories, shared while working the fields, remind her constantly of her origins. Such shared histories prove to be quite a grounding force in Tambu's life and are exactly what Nyasha loses touch with during her time in England. Connection to culture through such *oraliterature* insures a levelheadedness "[through] which Tambu makes clear, practical decisions about her feminine rebellion—this foundation in cultural practice proves invaluable" (Phillips 100). Having had such rich childhood literary experiences eventually enables Tambu to tell her own coherent story of "that process of expansion" as she does in *Nervous Conditions* (204).

Hard work and shared stories from the past, as we have seen, positively influence Tambu's self-formation allowing her to negotiate the divergent pieces of her self in the face of colonial and patriarchal dilemmas. In addition, a community of women surrounding her, encouraging her, challenging her, and helping her see the truth in often-muddled circumstances helps Tambu navigate her path as well. Tambu completes her narrative by referencing her helpful community:

"but the story I have told here, is my own story, the story of four women whom I loved, and our men" (204). Each woman mentioned in her concluding remark, her mother, her aunts Maiguru and Lucia, and her cousin Nyasha, play different roles in her life; yet their combined influences give rise to Tambu's identity. Sadly, the individual stories of these other four women, as previously addressed, relate desperation, subservience, dependence, and degradation—each character represents "identifiable forms of colonial experience . . . shaped by identifiable historical forces associated with colonialism" (Booker 199). Not surprisingly, the central protagonist and *Bildungsheld* "functions as a point of convergence of all these forces. [Tambu's] growth and maturation lead her by the end of the text to declare her independence from Western cultural domination; thus she can be taken as indicative of the maturation of Zimbabwe as a modern nation, demanding its independence from white colonial and neocolonial rule" (Booker 199). Solidarity with other women in her life offers Tambu strength and support not unlike what Emecheta's Adah finds at Pussy Cat Mansions. Nonetheless, even within the context of her communal support, Tambu, like her native Zimbabwe, becomes and remains separate and independent. In the end, she makes her own decisions not to be like the other four women in her life. She stands alone, autonomous and determined not to succumb to the web of powers that irreversibly entangle the other women.

Conclusion

At the beginning of the Dangarembga's novel, Tambu appears to be just another character awed by the materialism the Western world can offer. That she desires an education is never in doubt, but her fascination with the "been-to" status of her educated uncle's family and her perception of her uncle as divine prompt doubts about how serious Tambu will be when she has her chance at the mission school. Dangarembga's (and Tambu's) *récit* slows and lengthens as Babamukuru's car pulls onto the mission school grounds and readers receive a frame by frame description of the new environment. Practical questions and anticipatory thoughts flood the mind of the young *Bildungsheld*—Where would she sleep? And with whom? How would her life be different? She thinks about warm blankets and the life without chores before classes begin. She considers the fact that her schoolbooks would live on a bookshelf and stay clean and she too would stay clean because the mission had tubs large enough to sit in and wash. Having heard in detail from her brother about how life would be at the mission school, Tambu's anticipation level runs high, "I could not wait to enjoy these consequences of having acquired an education on Babamukuru's part, of being in the process of acquiring one in my case" (61). Tambu continues to idolize her uncle while secretly chastising her cousins for a seeming lack of appreciation and respect for their parents.

When Tambu is challenged by Babamukuru and reminded of how lucky she is to be at such a school, she responds positively and afterward "entered [the] bedroom vowing earnestly that [she] would be like Babamukuru: straight as an arrow, as steely and true" (88). However, over time and after multiple conversations with Nyasha concerning the family's experiences and how issues should be considered in shades other than simple black or white, after observing interactions within the family, particularly the fight between Babamukuru and his daughter when he calls her a whore for coming in late at night, and after Babamukuru insists that Jeremiah and Mainini go through a Christian marriage ceremony so that their relationship could finally be legitimized, Tambu comes to the realization that Babamukuru is "divine" just as the United Kingdom is "heaven" for Adah; in other words, not at all. The pressure to be a good African and a leader for his people in the eyes of the colonizers leaves Babamukuru with bad nerves. Drawing strength from the solid foundation of cultural wisdom established by her mother and grandmother, Tambu stands up to Babamukuru and to (neo)colonial and patriarchal structures and refuses to participate in or attend her parents' Christian wedding. Tambu admits that she had never stood up against anything since coming to the mission and although the thoughts of defying her uncle make her want to stay in bed all day—a nervous condition, albeit relatively minor, all her own—she asserts her own subjectivity and takes a stand.

In her story's conclusion, Tambu, prompted by her mother's diagnosis of the disease of "Englishness" as the cause of Nyasha's slow but steady wasting away, wonders if she too is doomed:

> Was I being careful enough? For I was beginning to have a suspicion,
> . . . that I had been too eager to leave the homestead and embrace the
> 'Englishness' of the mission; and after that the more concentrated
> 'Englishness' of Sacred Heart. . . . I told myself I was a much more
> sensible person than Nyasha, because I knew what could or couldn't
> be done. In this way, I banished the suspicion, buried it in the depths
> of my subconscious, and happily went back to Sacred Heart. (203)

Nevertheless, contemplation of her possible condition yields ultimately to an inner resolve never to succumb to indoctrination by Western ideologies. The adult Tambu understands now that her youth allowed her then to minimize concerns for herself and her potentially developing nervous conditions. With age, she is more careful:

> I was young then and able to banish things, but seeds do grow. Although I was not aware of it then, no longer could I accept Sacred Heart and what it represented as a sunrise on my horizon. Quietly, unobtrusively and extremely fitfully, something in my mind began to assert itself, to question things and refuse to be brainwashed, bringing me to this time when I can set down this story. (203-04)

While Tambu dearly loves the four female family members whose individual stories weave in and out of her own, she will not be them, individually or collectively. *Nervous Conditions* is a modern African *Bildungsroman* that traces the path of development of a young female protagonist. The events of Tambu's story relate the real complexities and intricacies through which an authentic self is formed. For her, the main challenges to her personal *Bildung* come about because she is a young woman who must constantly fight against patriarchal partialities and because she copes daily with the negative effects of colonialism Able, Hirsch and Langland's description of the female *Bildungsheld*'s path as a "developmental course [that] is more conflicted, less direct" applies aptly to Tambu's advancement as an individual despite her struggles. Like other *Bildung* protagonists, both male and female, Tambu learns, in Lorna Ellis's terms, to "work within the system" to maximize her opportunities. Tambu develops a critical view of her new world, she profits from the lessons of the world and the example of others around her and she gains an affirmative attitude toward life as a while, all of which figure prominently in Randolph Shaffner's qualities portrayed by the central protagonist of a *Bildungsroman*. Tambu will be more; she has been grounded in a firm foundation, stood her ground, told her story and through it all developed and asserted her individuality.

Notes

1 While many Post-Colonial critics disagree with Jameson's critique, more on his notion of "national allegory" can be found in "Third-World Literature in the Era of Multinational Capitalism" in *Social Text* vol. 15, 1986, 65-88. For more on Lukács's theory of "typicality" see *The Meaning of Contemporary Realism*. London: Merlin, 1963.
2 Novels presenting African emasculation in colonial context include Emecheta's *Second-Class Citizen*, *In the Ditch*, and *The Joys of Motherhood*; Beyala's *Le petit prince de Belleville*; Mariama Bâ's *Un chant éclarte*; Laye's *L'Enfant noir*.
3 For more on this concept see Teresa de Lauretis's explanation in chapter one of her *Feminist Studies/Critical Studies*, Bloomington: Indiana UP, 1986.

Chapter 5

Roused to Re-newed Understanding: Reading Calixthe Beyala's *Le petit prince de Belleville*

> *"The women have gutted themselves behind my back. They've taken*
> *off their pagnes and dressed themselves anew in muslin. They've re-*
> *moved the hair from under their armpits and shaved the pubic area.*
> *Nothing is called by its name anymore. . . . Woman has changed. She*
> *has exchanged her pagne for trousers. Listen to me once again."*
> Abdou Traoré, Calixthe Beyala's *Le petit prince de Belleville*

Although Calixthe Beyala has lived in France since 1978, she has hardly lost touch with her Cameroonian cultural roots. Likewise, her novels continue to reflect ongoing and ever-evolving notions of the political, social, and personal changes wrought by Western colonization in African countries and by immigration to Western cultures by African natives. Cameroon has a lengthy history of association with European countries, most of them not at all positive. Slave trade began when the Portugueuse made their way into the area in 1472. In the early nineteenth century, the British ravaged natural resources harvesting ivory and palm oil for their own benefit. Missionaries arrived in the 1850s and the Germans became involved in 1884 when, during the Berlin Conference, they proclaimed the coastal area in and around Douala as their protectorate. Germans reorganized Douala and completed infrastructure expansions. However, during World War I, French and British troops occupied the area and in 1919 France and England officially divided the country into two zones. On the whole, Cameroonians suffered socially and politically in subsequent years. In January 1960, the French zone became independent and in 1961 part of the British zone reached independence by incorporation into Nigeria while the other part united with the former French zone.

Born in 1961, Beyala joins the latest wave of African writers, those born immediately before, during or just after independence of the majority of African countries. By all accounts, Beyala had a difficult childhood and adolescence. Her lack of familial stability and her on again, off again educational opportunities inform much of her writing. In fact, her success as a writer rests primarily on her singular ability to expose the plight of African women who face multiple challenges at home and abroad during the colonial and post-colonial eras. Not surprisingly, such perspectives of African women's status at home and in France are centrally situated in all her works.

Beyala is categorized by Susan Arndt as a *radical* African feminist author for her unrelenting messages "that men (as a social group) inevitably and in principle discriminate against, oppress and mistreat women" (85). In addition to the author's preoccupations with feminine development and emancipation, Arndt points to evidence in Beyala's depictions of "men characters [who] are, 'by nature' or because of their socialization, hopelessly sexist and usually deeply immoral" (85). Even though Arndt's classification is based principally on her novels *C'est le soleil qui m'a brulée* and *Tu t'appelleras Tanga*, other critics such as Clément Mbom acknowledge a multiplicity of themes tied to and emanating from Beyala's overarching preoccupation with the status of women:

> Lorsqu'on observe le contenu de ses œuvres, une constatation semble s'imposer: il n'existe pas de thème central jouant un double rôle centrifuge et centripète. On assiste plutôt à une multiplicité, à une variation, à une prolifération de thèmes. A partir d'un sujet, d'autres sujets se greffent qui, à leur tour, font naître des thèmes variés, souvent secondaires.
>
> Pourtant tous ces sujets tournent autour d'un dénominateur commun: la condition de la femme africaine, la condition de la femme camerounaise. Ce thème structurateur de toute sa création romanesque actuelle connaît une évolution et un approfondissement du premier au dernier ouvrage en date. (52)

> [When one observes the content of her works, one might note that a centralized or centripetal theme does not exist. One experiences rather a multiplicity, a variation, a proliferation of themes. To a given

subject, others attached themselves one by one, give birth to other, often secondary themes.
Nevertheless, all these themes revolve around one common denominator: the African woman's condition, the Cameroonian woman's condition. This organizing theme, of all other current novelistic creations, evolves and deepens from the first to the last of her works to date.]

Beyala is without question a different kind of novelist compared to Emecheta and Dangarembga and not just for reasons associated with African feminism. The playful recounting of the Belleville novels combined with fresh choices of narrative voicing belies the intense subject matter at the heart of each work. Unfortunately, Beyala has been the subject of unfavorable criticism as well. She has been accused of plagiarizing Howard Buten's *Quand j'avais 5 ans je m'ai tué* and Romain Gary's *La vie devant soi* in *Le petit prince de Belleville*. Her novel was subsequently ordered out of print by a judge. Likewise, she was accused of plagiarizing Ben Okri's *The Famished Road* in *Les honneurs perdus* (1996). Beyala refuses these accusations and is supported in her work by many scholars and critics such as Mireille Rosello who reads the novels in question intertextually, in the same manner that Beyala's novel can be read intertextually with *Le petit prince* by Saint-Exupéry.

Both Belleville novels, *Le petit prince de Belleville* and *Maman a un amant*, feature a double-stranded narrative. The principal narratives in the two novels are recounted by the young son of a Malian family recently relocated to France. Readers often wonder why Beyala chooses to tell the story of a Malian family since she is herself from Cameroon. Perhaps one explanation is that she might be in a better position to recount the social, racial and gender difficulties of life within a post-colonial context if she is able to distance herself from the individual characters by changing their nationality; in other words, making them Malian instead of Cameroonian. In any case, Loukoum chronicles the activities of the Traorés as they try to live traditional lives in Belleville, an immigrant community in northeast Paris. When viewed through the eyes of a quirky yet observant adolescent, the blending of immigrant cultures and traditions with the social realities of modern France produces often humorous and always telling insights. In *Le petit prince*, the chief story line is interrupted at practically every chapter division with the philosophical musings on life as an immigrant on the soil of the former colonizer by Abdou, Loukoum's father. In *Maman*, it is M'am, Loukoum's adopted mother and Abdou's oldest wife who intermittently shares her interior thoughts. Such an alternation in narrative voice in each book allows for reflective insights of the two principal adult characters; the first, Abdou, miserable because of his new living circumstances and the second, M'am, realistic and clear-sighted about her personal situation, while a child, Loukoum, relates with humor and naïveté the day to day events he and his family experience.

One of the chief characteristics of the traditional *Bildungsroman* is that the work traces the organic development of a young child as he experiences life and is educated both formally and informally. In fact, Jerome H. Buckley's *Season of Youth* focuses exclusively on the magical adolescent period of growth and enlightenment in novels influenced by Goethe and written by English authors from Dickens to Golding. As alluded to in the Chapter One of this study, the period of youth presents a myriad of dynamic moments when children can learn, experience things, face challenges, make decisions, take up an art, and confront their parents as they make a "conscious attempt . . . to integrate [their] powers [and] to cultivate [themselves] by . . . experience" (Howe 6). The three novels discussed here in Chapters Two, Three and Four as Post-colonial *Bildungsromane* feature two female children, Adah and Tambu, who undergo various experiences and their own kind of *Bildung* akin to, yet distinct from, development traced in more traditional texts of the genre. Ironically, Beyala's texts, because of their male protagonist and narrator, appear to revert to the more traditional *Bildungsroman* structure and this from an author who has been categorized as a radical writer at many levels. Indeed, surface analyses of *Le petit prince* and *Maman* chronicle the development of a young immigrant boy who seeks to reconcile his life experiences in Mali with what he discovers life to be like in France, but under the surface Beyala's project is in these two novels rewrites the traditional male *Bildungsroman* for a new time and a new culture. Based on the author's treatment of similar subject matter presented in other novels and the innovative narrative techniques successfully mastered in the Belleville novels (especially those in *Maman* featuring M'am), Beyala is truly writing a modern female novel of awakening, a specific type of modern *Bildungsroman*.

A Traditional Bildungsroman?

> "*J'ai mis un enfant au centre de mon livre, parce que les mots d'un enfant ont quelque chose de magique, de fantastique.*"[1]
> Calixthe Beyala

> ["*I put a child at the center of my book, because the words of a child have something magical about them, something fantastic.*"]

Loukoum, "seven years old, but in Africa . . . ten seasons old" recounts in often humorous detail the ins and outs of life for the adults and children around him (de Jager 1). Loukoum observes and reflects upon daily interactions and situations. Like various heroes in traditional novels of development, Loukoum learns and grows, has the opportunity to acquire a formal education even though it is at times frustrating because of his socio-economic status, experiences what he believes to be true love while facing intergenerational tensions with his own parents and with the parents of the object of his affection, Lolita. Additionaly, he is the author of his own story; the autobiographer of a book that he believes one day will be made into a movie. Beyala takes great pains to express the thoughts and imagination of her young protagonist.

Beyala's well-calculated objective to consider life and love, issues and dynamics of gender, as well as the interactions of individuals in post-colonial contexts is not only successful, but, because of the inventive narrative technique and choice of male narrator, outright inventive when compared to her contemporaries. Regarding this narrative, Jean-Marie Volet asserts:

> The discovery of the world through a child's eyes is nothing new. The publisher's reference to Le Petit Nicolas and Zazie, two well-known characters of French literature, indicates this[2]. So too does the very title of Beyala's novel, which parodies Saint-Exupéry's celebrated *Petit Prince*. Nevertheless, very few successes stand out along this well-trodden path, and many attempts by adults to recapture the spirit of youth have ended in dismal failure. Such is not the case with Beyala's novel, which provides a convincing blend of narrative complexity, irony, and false candor tailored to specific literary expectations of both writer and reader. (311)

There is certainly a sense that Beyala's writing is for her a kind of therapy or catharsis. Long a resident of the same neighborhood her characters here inhabit, Beyala appears to be coming to her own terms with the dynamics of life in another land as she follows the lives of her fictional characters. Additionally and perhaps more evidently, the author allows her readers access to the complex happenings in the lives of immigrants in the Belleville quarter of Paris and by extension the Western world. Beyala's skill at crystallizing the predicament of Africans living in other cultures is finely calibrated and yields incisive truths despite the initial inexperience and naïveté of the voice through which the larger part of the story is relayed. In this vein, Volet continues: "At no time is the reader allowed to gain the impression that the writer is only telling a childish . . . story, and at no time does the reader get the impression that the author has fallen victim to her own game and slipped into the gentle mood of Utopian innocence. Loukoum's view of the world fuels irony and allows the author to savage many *idées reçues*" (311). Indeed, Loukoum finds himself in a multitude of telling and unexpected situations and he never hesitates to share his thoughts and perspectives freely and candidly.

In *Le petit prince*, interactions between the young Malian immigrant and adults are ubiquitous. Of course there are those between himself and his parents, extended family, and classmates, but Loukoum is also exposed during his development to prostitutes (including his own biological mother), Madame Saddock, a feminist French social worker, teachers, and neighboring African immigrants. Like the traditional *Bildungsroman* hero, Loukoum is depicted as, if not completely at odds with preceding generations, at least dubious about their behavior and demands of him. A striking example is seen early in the novel when Loukoum grapples with his opportunity for education and his teacher Mademoiselle Garnier. Concerned because her immigrant student can neither read nor write standard French, Mlle. Garnier presses the issue and Loukoum reflects:

> They're funny these teachers, I don't know how it works but they're all the same. They always ask you the same questions and when you want to explain to them that we are taught the Koran, and that the Koran contains all there is to know on earth, and that the father gets Allah's advice, and that I don't need to learn anything anyway because it's the women who'll be doing the work for me, they look at each other, shake their heads, and say: 'Oh! How awful. The poor kid!' (de Jager 2)

After he struggles through an excerpt of Saint-Exupéry's *Le petit prince*, Mlle. Garnier quickly discovers that Loukoum cannot read French and she suspects that his reading ability in Arabic may be little more than memorized religious passages from the Koran. Loukoum excuses his lack of ability in French by telling his teacher that "It wasn't so much that the words were difficult, but the guy who wrote it had words a mile long, words that went on and on and on" (de Jager 3). There is no doubt that school is a struggle both academically and socially for Loukoum; however, he perseveres and takes advantage of help from a classmate, Pierre Pelletier, who not only becomes Loukoum's primary academic support, but a terrific encourager as well.

In a twist of irony befitting such an unpredictable author, Loukoum profits in his informal training by unlikely relationships with prostitutes. One of the first occasions in which a prostitute figures in his life is the special outing to a swimming pool Mademoiselle Esther proposes. At once, Loukoum is fascinated by Esther and everything associated with her. It is as if all that surrounds her suddenly becomes magical. Ironically, Beyala, for her part, allows her chosen narrator, a young boy, to express his sexist and emerging misogynistic views freely. After what amounts to a modified peep show for Loukoum where Esther twirls around in a scanty bathing suit, Esther demonstrates various swimming techniques and strokes. Needless to say, Loukoum becomes excited about being able to meet again for future lessons:

> 'It's really very nice of you to teach me how to swim. . . . Do you think we can come back again?'
> 'Of course! Why not? With all those guys sticking their thing up you, a little exercise and some fresh air won't do me any harm.'
> I didn't really understand what she meant, but in any case it doesn't make any difference considering I think she's splendid, and if you have the luck to have a girl of that calibre to teach you how to swim, so much the better for you. (de Jager 38-9)

With Mademoiselle Esther, Loukoum perceives his surroundings differently offering new perspectives and stimulating his personal development. For instance, through Loukoum's eyes the park they visit after swimming lessons and lunch transforms itself into a sort of Garden of Eden. Loukoum remarks: "As soon as we walked into the park, I inhaled the air. It was as if we were some-where else . . . Everything around us was green . . . Even the sun, you'd have thought this was the place it was born and would go to sleep" (de Jager 39). Esther is not the only prostitute to play an important, albeit brief, role in the de-velopment of this young Malian.

Loukoum's biological mother Aminata is also a prostitute. Although he is being raised by his father and the latter's two wives, M'am and Soumana, Loukoum's biological mother appears at the door one day wishing to spend time with her son. Her knock at the door of the Traoré's apartment introduces yet another growth opportunity for Loukoum. Aminata, regretful for being separated from her son for several years, now wants to play a role in his life and part of that role would involve giving him the experience of life away from the apart-ment. According to Aminata: "All our great men, Mitterrand, de Gaulle, Sen-ghor, Delon, Frank Sinatra, Martin Luther King, all of them grew up on a farm. Think about it, it's ideal for a kid: feeding the chickens, geese, ducks, milking the cows, horse-riding" (de Jager 146). Although her idea of a *séjour* in the countryside is just a ruse to convince Abdou to let her take her son away for a few days, Loukoum does indeed stretch his imagination and learn a lot from his mother. Their time together is one of happiness as they fantasize about moving to Canada and about the prospects of building a house on the moon. Loukoum is enthralled by his mother's vivacity and whimsy and being out of his father's apartment and from under his despotic control proves to be not only diversion-ary, but also quite instructional. His transformation continues as he experiences life outside of familial restrictions.

Traditional *Bildungsromane* often feature the hero's first sexual encounters. Although Beyala's young protagonist does not engage in conventional inter-course, he and his schoolmate crush, Lolita, do playfully explore one another. Loukoum tells us that "Lolita had a room all to herself with white curtains and a beautiful bedspread with birds of paradise on which I didn't dare sit. First we played with a puzzle. Then we played mummies and daddies, the game I like best" (de Jager 106). This incident is one of several occurrences that leads to Lolita's move to a different school. Nevertheless, she constantly remains on Loukoum's mind and throughout the remainder of the novel he thinks of her and wonders where she is and what she is doing. Near the end of the novel, as his familial life appears to improve, he still reflects on their time together and won-ders if fate would ever allow their togetherness:

> I think of Lolita. I'm sad. I'm unhappy. Especially when I see a girl
> walking along and I think it's her. I remember her hair, the rain out-
> side, the rain beating down, her fingers running round, cuddly fin-
> gers. I remember everything. And everything comes back. . . . If Lo-
> lita writes to me I'll be in seventh heaven. . . . Keep your mind busy
> while you wait, I tell myself. That's what I have to learn about life: to
> fill the gap. (de Jager 173)

When Lolita does eventually write, Loukoum is so afraid to read the letter that he stashes it away. He feels he would be unable to live if Lolita were to reveal that she no longer loves him. Not knowing anything from Lolita is better in Loukoum's mind than knowing what he fears might be the status of their relationship. After being unable to sleep however, his curiosity triumphs and he reads his love's letter. By the second sentence, Lolita reveals her continued love and affection for him. Loukoum becomes ecstatic and his thoughts fast forward immediately to eventual marriage and children:

> Lord! when I finish reading Lolita's letter, my whole body is hot. I'm beginning to spin around and around. I can't stay in one place. I raise my arms to the sky. Thank you, Lord, for having given me Lolita. Then I sit down in a corner, put my head on my knees. I weep. I imagine Lolita all alone on her bed. She stays awake for the same reasons. I weep some more. I'm dripping with tears. Lord! Yes, we'll be married! We'll have kids! (de Jager 175)

At the close of the first Belleville novel, Beyala's hero has grown, has had significant life experiences and has loved in meaningful ways. In addition, like the heroes of traditional *Bildungsromane*, Loukoum develops in intellect and knowledge.

Although Loukoum faces difficulties early in his schooling, he perseveres, learns good French and much more. He has a competent teacher who is aware of his gradual progress, but it is his classmate, Pierre Pelletier, who really helps him to succeed academically. Loukoum realizes that his formal education will not come easily, but he knows that Pierre "is a good schoolteacher. He is really wicked that kid. He makes me read . . . Pierre Pelletier's other name is patience" (de Jager 45). Pierre appears not only to be successful in his academic tutoring, but also in his ability to inspire Loukoum to be a high achiever. Loukoum is motivated by Pierre's challenge "'You've got to struggle,'. . . . 'You must! You must!' (de Jager 45). Indeed, Loukoum makes progress at school, but, and perhaps this is more important, he grows in wisdom through his observation and scrutiny of the world around him.

Beyala's double-stranded narrative featuring both the philosophical musings of Loukoum's father and the principal narrative by Loukoum has been addressed earlier in this chapter. So far, however, discussion has been centered on Loukoum's *récit*. Abdou's contributions to the story, although much shorter, communicate great insights into the dynamics of *Bildung*, but also the effects of colonialism on an immigrant family. This Malian father's thoughts indicate the superior role that he feels he is supposed to play in his family. Knowing Beyala's penchant for authoring revolutionary texts, readers know right away that she is about something else here as well. Odile Cazenave asserts that "Beyala offers a new access to man's consciousness," and it is evident that this consciousness readily reveals masculine weakness (*Rebellious Women . . .* 180). Cazenave also notes that in Beyala "[m]an has actually adopted the language of the victim, a language typically associated with woman" (*Rebellious Women . . .* 174). Such language and mindset are the products of constant power struggles between former colonizers and formerly colonized individuals. Désirée Lewis, basing her analysis on the theories of Frantz Fanon[3] and others, suggests that the presence of Western white males causes a change in the African male's subjectivity. She writes that "black men's construction by a white power structure is seen to engender a split self and a conflict between invisibility and manhood" (Lewis 46). Likewise, Alain-Philippe Durand writes "Cette appartenance quasi exclusive du père aux coutumes de son pays natal se traduit dans le roman par sa réserve, voire son silence, dans l'espace migratoire" (54) ["The father's quasi-exclusive belonging to his native country's customs translates in the novel by his reserve, witness his silence, in the migratory space"]. Abdou struggles futilely to maintain a unified self while living day to day under Western influence.

While Abdou fully comprehends the importance of passing on a certain heritage to his son, he knows that Loukoum must be prepared to receive his "possessions." He tells his son: "Listen, Loukoum, you're my heir. One day, all that I have will be yours. So listen carefully" (de Jager 58). However, Abdou progressively becomes aware of his fleeting influence over his offspring and his own growing debility. Speaking to his unidentified "friend," a singular representation of the collective colonizer, Abdou acknowledges:

> But you know, friend, little by little my son was no longer listening to me. Or when he lent me an ear it was with a pout, the pout of a television announcer.
> I've known the tragedies of my religion for too long. I've struggled alone for too long against Christianity.
> Today I see my son.
> He has discovered the vocabulary of Paris. Words scratched in by wind and weather.
> He has acquired other ways of saying hello.
> He knows rituals that throw me.
> He feels repugnance at eating with his hands.
> He imposes other conformities.
> He imports tastes, preoccupations...
> Friend my son no longer listens to me. I feel emptied of myself, robbed and ransacked of my last dream, to the last of what is beautiful . . .
> I believe I'm going mad. (de Jager 144)

It is clear here and in several other places in Abdou's remarks that he is well aware of the evolving separation between himself and his son. Thus readers have still another indication that Loukoum is developing into his own selfhood, undergoing his own *Bildung*. He will be his own individual although it is not yet clear whether he will be a repressor like his father or whether he will resist the patriarchal sway and be understanding toward women.

As with the traditional *Bildungsroman* hero, Loukoum's process of self-realization is influenced by a wide array of external factors. As he makes contact with the outside world, he unfolds as an individual. Without a doubt he belongs socially and culturally to "a whole tribe of niggers," (de Jager 47 sic) as he puts it again and again, but his observations and experiences in Belleville allow for an independent self-formation while catalyzing an eagerness for and excitement about learning how life works. Time and time again, Loukoum hypothesizes about the ways of people and the ways of the world. Gloria Nne Onyeoziri mentions the following specific areas:

> Par son procédé d'apprentissage, qui consiste à tout dire au hazard, Loukoum se concentre sur les différents maux du monde: l'oppression comme un phénomène mondial dans les rapports de force, tel que l'expulsion des autochtones de leur terre (aux Amériques), l'oppression violente des femmes qui ont comme juge leur propre assassin . . . , les tirailleurs noirs qui, ruinés physiquement par la guerre, reçoivent pour toute récompense des décorations et de médailles . . . , les femmes africaines qui sont démunies de tout espoir d'épanouissement. . . . Loukoum souligne l'attitude irrespectueuse de son père envers les femmes, tout en faisant la même chose à sa façon. (12)

Loukoum witnesses and observes, gives commentary on various behaviors and reports on real life situations and circumstances so much so that Cazenave has been prompted to classify him as "le nouveau griot moderne de la famille" ["the new and modern *griot* of the family"] ("Calixthe Beyala: l'exemple d'une écriture décentrée . . . " 126). In this role, he is capable of accomplishing at least three important things at once for the reader.

First, Loukoum's progression toward self-development becomes more and more clarified for the reader. As the narrative advances readers can effortlessly chart Loukoum's *Bildung*. On occasion, he plainly analyzes his status on the path to development. Perhaps the clearest expression of all that Loukoum has learned and all he still needs to learn comes after Abdou is released from prison. Loukoum observes major changes of demeanor in his father, but is generally pleased with the latter's reincorporation into the family home as Abdou becomes more loving toward M'am and the rest of the family than ever before. However, he admits other things trouble him:

> I have many questions that bother me a great deal. I wonder why love makes us suffer? Why the earth is round? Why are there stars? Why laughter, trouble, and joy? Why the different races? What purpose does it all serve, these differences that hurt and cause so much uproar? I realize that school has taught me many things without ever giving answers to what is essential. I still have quite a bit of work to do. (de Jager 173)

Even though Loukoum's narrative often drips with false candor which Beyala uses to demonstrate the depths of her principal narrator's mischief and his independent spirit, he here demonstrates maturity and unflinching honesty in the estimation of his own abilities. Undoubtedly, Loukoum's development is in progress and what he will be like in the end, whether or not he will end up like his father, is still in question.

Second, the reader is presented with seemingly innocent yet frighteningly revealing observations. While Beyala's choice of this young, male narrative voice, the one who not only recounts the series of events and interprets the interactions of people around him but who apparently learns and grows from what he witnesses, seems peculiar given the author's earlier works [*C'est le soleil qui m'a brulée* and *Tu t'appelleras Tanga*] and her overall feminist ideology; but the manner in which she uses her narrator, according to Cazenave, "permet à l'auteur de mettre à plat certains aspects de la vie africaine mal compris, mal perçues par la société française" ["permits the author to lay open certain poorly understood and poorly perceived aspects of African life by French society"] ("Calixthe Beyala: l'exemple d'une écriture décentrée . . . " 127).

Third, Beyala uses the perspectives of this young Malian male to highlight the conditions of her female characters. According to Cazenave "Sous couvert d'une voix pseudo-enfantine, Beyala nous transmit des observations à chaud, sans, en apparence, tirer de conclusion" ("Calixthe Beyala: l'exemple d'une écriture décentrée . . . " 128). ["Under cover of a pseudo-childlike voice, Beyala communicates on the spot observations, without, apparently drawing conclusions".] *Le petit prince*, despite its male narrators and the fact that observations are set forth without qualification, is not as much about masculine perspectives as it is about the social, cultural, and gender specific challenges of African women living in the West. Earlier in this chapter, remarks were set forth asserting the possibility of Beyala's reversion to the more traditional *Bildungsroman* structure in chronicling the life of her young male protagonist. While this case can certainly be made based on superficial evidence, I contend that Beyala is up to much more especially as *Le petit prince* and *Maman* are considered more closely and in tandem. The feminist themes of her previous texts and the fact that she uses inventive narrative techniques in these two novels point to a project that is much more ideologically and theoretically unconventional: Beyala is truly writing a modern female novel of awakening, a specific type of modern *Bildungsroman*.

The Novel of Awakening

Susan J. Rosowski's and Rita Felski's conceptions of growth and development for fictional female characters take into account the realities of life for women who unavoidably reside within patriarchal societies. Rosowski, nonetheless, clings to the importance of what she terms a process of awakening for some female characters which is characterized by "movement [that] is inward, toward greater self-knowledge that leads in turn to a revelation of the disparity between that self-knowledge and the nature of the world" (Rosowski 49). Rosowski's theory draws upon Western works such as Gustave Flaubert's *Madame Bovary*, Kate Chopin's *The Awakening*, and George Eliot's *Middlemarch*, but can prove insightful when applied to Beyala's central female character in the Belleville novels, M'am. Once more, the intention here is not to impose Western literary theory on African texts without proper justification. While African fictional female characters do face added racial, class, and cultural biases while living as immigrants in the West, they do share the effects of similar gender biases with women around the world. Patriarchy predominates be it in Nigeria, Zimbabwe, Mali, France or the United States. Thus it is due to the shared circumstances women endure because of masculinist power paradigms and points of reference that an amalgamation of Rosowski's and Felski's theories will be invoked here. Rosowski proposes that novels of awakening distinguish themselves from traditional *Bildungsromane* by the ways in which the protagonist develops or arrives at understanding and self-recognition. First and foremost, the individual undergoing personal *Bildung* in novels of awakening are always female and quite often older than the developing individuals in the majority of conventional *Bildungsromane*. It appears in some instances that more extensive life experiences, due simply to the fact that the protagonist is older, than those available to Emecheta's Adah and Dangarembga's Tambu or Nyasha trigger in the heroine the process of awakening. Rosowski notes that "the direction of awakening follows what is becoming a pattern in literature by and about women. The protagonist's growth results typically not with 'an art of living,' as for her male counterpart, but instead with a realization that for a woman such an art of living is difficult or impossible: it is an awakening to limitations" (49). Other characteristics are general and may not apply to every novel of awakening.

Many novels of awakening feature protagonists who come to realize their inner longing for freedom from the restraints traditionally placed on women by society. Often, according to Rosowski, women sacrifice love relationships in their quest to sate their desire for personal freedom (64). Women in novels of awakening come to realize that life might offer more than a romanticized existence or questionable familial support and often they choose to remove themselves from the "comforts" of customary surroundings which could include leaving a husband or lover, leaving the town for the country or generally disconnecting themselves from the familiar. Rita Felski's notion of the novel of awakening, a term she admits borrowing from Rosowski and then adapting, differs somewhat from Rosowski's[4]. Felski believes that "self-discovery is achieved through a process of withdrawal and reflection, during which the heroine intuitively becomes aware of an essential female identity" (141). She regards the process as one that directs the individual back to an original moment. As Felski insists,

> The *telos* of the novel refers back to a point of origin; the goal of fe-
> male identity is perceived as inherently present, waiting only to be
> discovered. Hence the circular structure of the genre; female self is
> frequently envisaged as an authentic centre which has accrued layers
> of false consciousness, rather than a goal to be attained over time—as
> a primary metaphysical self from which the protagonist has become
> estranged. The act of emancipation requires an escape from history, a
> return to an identity understood as prior in both a historical and phi-
> losophical sense. . . . The heroine must become what she once was,
> recover an identity which is complete and self-contained, rather than
> contingent, and historically and socially determined. (141)

In order then for awakening to occur, the protagonist must shed layers of socially determined identities not inherently her own. Such liberation allows for
new understanding and authentic self-recognition even if for a limited time. Because all heroines, regardless of race or class, are similarly affected, it is crucial
to expose and examine the greater contention, which is even more noteworthy
than a ten year old boy's *Bildung*, in Beyala's works, that of the standing, potential, and opportunity for liberating a Malian woman residing in France.

The Prince's Mother—Debunking Stereotypes on Paths to Understanding Anew

> *"Et moi, j'ai choisi de travailler sur l'individu, non pas sur la masse;
> la masse, ça ne m'intéresse pas. Et ça c'est très nouveau pour
> l'Afrique."*
>
> [*"As for me, I chose to focus on the individual, not on the masses;
> The masses, they do not interest me. And that is very new for Af-
> rica."*]
> –Calixthe Beyala in a 1993 interview conducted by Françoise Cévaër

Beyala's main concern in the two Belleville novels is M'am's awakening to
re-newed understanding concerning her promise and potential even within the
context of patriarchal and post-colonial power structures which have seemingly
squelched any hope of personal agency. Abdou's first wife, Maryam or M'am
for short, is a dedicated woman, about 50 years old, whose patience and perseverance with her husband and family up to the time the narrative begins in *Le
petit prince* have been remarkable. Beyala aspires to instill a consciousness in
her audience of the day to day realities within the African family unit by ad-
dressing questions of sexuality: in particular questions of polygamy as well as of
gender roles and prostitution. Although she does not approve of Abdou's behavior, M'am takes it in stride and makes the best of a messy and often embarassing
situation while her co-wife Soumana rages against such masculine injustice and

egotism. Additionally, as noted earlier in this chapter, Aminata, the biological mother of Abdou's son Loukoum, is a prostitute; Abdou agrees to raise his son and M'am agrees to help care for him. In fact, Loukoum, as well as other children living in the home have been unofficially listed as belonging to the infertile M'am for reasons of welfare allocations. It appears that everything has been worked out, but after officials learn of Abdou's fraudulence, he is sent to prison. Many of Beyala's depictions of home and family life diverge from utopic portrayals presented by other African authors such as Camara Laye. In general the complexity and chaos of such home life, while not necessarily out of place in Belleville, would appear perilous to most Parisians, especially social workers like Madame Saddock who for a time routinely comes around to check on the well-being of the women in the household. Through all of these difficulties, Beyala demonstrates how M'am can awaken to feminine potential even though permanent access to such expansion eludes her for now.

In *Le petit prince*, Beyala constructs her characters in order to expose subverted selves which embody alternate roles and gender qualities. Her scrutiny of the African immigrant family in France exposes the fluidity of sexual selfhood and problematizes traditional gender construction. The immigrant community provides the setting wherein Western and African morés and values constantly rub against each other. On the surface, Beyala's renderings of the roles and responsibilities of each family member align with stereotyped constructions. For instance, she portrays the male head-of-household, Abdou, who busies himself solely with matters of public life and who provides financially for his family. The author presents the female who tends to matters of the home and children and who obeys the wishes of her husband. While rejecting perspectives mainstream Western feminism might promote, Beyala tantalizes her readers in the first volume with a presentation of a heroine who not only challenges codified gender constructions and begins to sense liberation from Felski's "layers of false consciousness," but who awakens for a short time at least to an alternative selfhood in *Maman*. This precarious balance of exposing stereotypes while at the same time subverting them reveals the extent to which Beyala's representation of the potentials of women pushes constructions of selfhood to new limits.

M'am proves to be an excellent adoptive mother to young Loukoum. Even though she cannot conceive children herself, she shows no anger or bitterness toward raising another woman's child. Essentially neglected by Abdou (until after his time in prison), M'am devotedly busies herself with endless domestic chores without much complaint. In addition, she is the chief caregiver for Soumana, her younger, but ailing and frustrated co-wife. Cazenave adds that M'am remains faithful to religious commandments and even though Abdou sleeps around she knows he will eventually come back. Soumana belongs to a younger generation and "accepting Abdou's behavior is out of the question" (Cazenave, *Rebellious Women* . . . 184). Cazenave raises a critical point with her analysis of Abdou's wives. Noting that Soumana loses her appetite, grows weak, and risks losing her life, she posits that in Soumana's mind "Abdou has to choose between her and other women. M'am," Cazenave continues, "believes that La Soumana['s] response is a mistake. They must not do anything to push the man away" (*Rebellious Women* . . . 184). Cazenave concludes with the following questions and a revealing comment: "Is this wisdom or resignation? Should one be tolerant (in order to have peace) or tempestuous (and lose one's illusions)? In this context, La Soumana's death is symbolic of the inevitable suffering of the woman who puts all her hope in love" (*Rebellious Women* . . . 184). In contrast, M'am perseveres through Abdou's unfaithfulness and when Soumana's life is over, M'am is still around to grow and develop even if in limited ways. M'am does not put "all her hope in love," but instead she relies on her inner strength and desires to press toward self-individuation. As we will soon see, M'am refuses to rely on Abdou for her own well being; she carves her own path toward female awakening.

Theorist Nancy Chodorow maintains that "mothering is a rich experience, but simultaneously traps women into a different adult role from that of men, one which is not as well rewarded in contemporary society" (Walby 94). The degree to which M'am and Soumana have been debased by patriarchal privilege evinces itself throughout. The sad reality of the lives of these women and their foremothers is exhibited in an exchange one day between the two:

> How many kids did she have, your mother?
> 'Dunno. The wives, there were thirty of them. And each one must have given birth six times at least. You figure it out.'
> 'And how were they together?'
> 'They worked in the fields and then, to get that out of their minds, they would fight with each other all the time and bully each other's children just to get back at my dad. Me, I used to think they should have united against him and beat him up until they killed him. But instead they allowed him to reign over them like a lord. Little did I know then I would be living the same dog's life.' (de Jager 34)

As the novel progresses, the proof of the deplorable conditions of this "vie de chien" which M'am and other African women live is made manifest. Beyala's descriptions communicate the difficulties and the harshness of the feminine condition. After Soumana becomes too sick to help with domestic chores, everything falls to M'am. Yet Beyala gives readers a signal that even in times of desperation and exhaustion this *Bildungsheld* understands that there is still potential in her life, that she can grow and develop and become. Loukoum ponders: "Since Soumana's illness, all the work falls on M'am's shoulders. She washes, she sings, she cleans, she sings, she irons, she sings, she cooks, she sings. I always wonder why tired people sing so much. M'am told me it's because they have nothing else to do" (de Jager 123). Loukoum's contemplation seems quite simple, too simple in fact. How could a feminist writer like Beyala lead her readers to believe, even momentarily, that her female protagonist will accept so easily and without contention what seems to be not only her destiny but the destiny of all women? The answer is that Beyala cannot and she will not.

While the text seems to present the clichéd story of immigrant female characters trapped in polygamous marriages and fated to lives of servitude, Beyala, on closer observation, proposes something fresh and original. In a 1992 interview with Narcisse Kombi, Beyala contends: "J'ai toujours prôné la supériorité de la femme. Je ne peux me départir de cette conception. L'Afrique ne serait pas l'Afrique sans ses femmes. La femme, avec tout ce qu'elle produit comme travail, est le moteur de ce continent" (Online Interview). ["I have always preached the superiority of woman. I cannot veer from this conception. Africa would not be Africa without its women. Woman, with all she produces through her efforts, is the motor of this continent."] Beyala does not allow M'am's desperation to get the best of her while reminding her readers that history has shown woman's inherent strength in the face of obstacles and her potential for self-formation. Once again Lorna Ellis's notion of growing down to grow up applies[5]. Ellis discusses authors who create female *Bildung* protagonists who "work within the limits of their societies, . . . [and authors, who like Beyala,] allow their heroines to mature or 'grow up'—to understand themselves and their relationship to their environment, and to negotiate that environment in order to maintain some form of agency" (18). Despite her condition, M'am holds a certain qualified power. For instance, if the discourse from the quotation regarding singing is reexamined and taken further, the protagonist's strength is revealed:

> M'am is very sweet. Never raises her voice, not one single loud word. She doesn't even complain about the work. She just works. She finds pretexts to say something nice to each kid. I swear this woman has happiness running through her body. One day, I asked her this question: 'Why're you always happy, M'am?' ''Cause happiness, son, is like good health. It's when you don't feel anything anymore.'
> (de Jager 123)

M'am knows how to transcend the initial oppression brought on specifically by her husband but also by the biases inherent in all social contexts. She gets on by making the best of a life that seems to offer only the worst of circumstances. Jean-Marie Volet notes that,

> even when [Beyala's characters] are roughed up by life, failed by society, and threatened with annihilation, most of [them] survive the bruising of their bodies and the torments imposed upon their minds. Battered but eventually liberated, they then feel free and able to reinvent the meaning of life before moving toward the dim glow of hope shining on the horizon of their future. (309)

M'am's mental and emotional preparations, her singing and her outward cheerfulness, allow her to face her environment and to cope, in some senses, with constraints imposed on her by patriarchal society. In addition, M'am appears to possess a subtle power, which tilts the advantage in her favor. Cazenave notes the almost Senghorian poetic à la "Femme Noire" at work in Abdou's ruminations and the dependence in Loukoum even when he knows that "certain things [he] shouldn't do [for M'am] because [he is] a man" (de Jager 142). Here, Cazenave posits, woman emerges as "savior," as "the only anchoring point in this unknown world of change and wandering" (*Rebellious Women . . .* 174). Abdou lives with an admiration for women while lamenting his growing powerlessness in their presence. For him, women are alluring and mystifying. Early in the novel, he states:

> So I curl up in those magical sheets in which woman weaves me
> thousands of dreams, on the other side of the wounds. She teaches me
> the legends anew and I ejaculate my tenderness in the wind.
> Woman is my drug. I will never be tired of it.
> Fragile hours resounding with hope, . . .
> The body of woman is my heaven, my wealth, my permanent mira-
> cle. (de Jager 65)

Abdou's enchantment with women is obvious; yet a tension between his enthrallment with women and his shrinking "authority" in their presence manifests itself. Later in the novel he proclaims "I'm falling like a stone into a black well which is undoubtedly death. In my head is emptiness or else a fat black cloud. I've lost my memory. And what is all this for? I have wives who'll end up strangling me in my sleep. I have a son in whom I shall not be continued" (de Jager 156). Abdou's transformation is the inverse of M'am's. According to Cazenave: "The father's departure (when he is arrested by the authorities) and subsequent return bring about a radical change in their lives. M'am subsequently runs the house and holds the power, and so she is also in charge of the game of love" (185). Volet concurs: "As the power of Loukoum's father diminishes, the women around him begin to take things in their own hands. There is no doubt that the move toward liberation springs from a pragmatic attempt to make the best of life in the difficult circumstances rather than from a deliberate attempt to run for freedom. Even so, the result cannot be minimized" (312). Beyala subverts traditional gender roles to emphasize M'am's growing awareness of selfhood. She focuses on Abdou's shrinking power while pointing out M'am's emerging potential. Beyala describes the situation through Loukoum's young eyes:

> M'am has no longer the same appearance. She wears trousers, blue,
> yellow, red ones with matching sandals. She looks younger, more
> carefree. My dad, he's looking for something. You'd think he was
> studying nature. The other day he brought a plant home. He's taking
> care of it, feeds it, as if it were a baby. He even brought flowers home
> for M'am. Monsieur Guillaume says that he is searching for God in
> woman. He buys plenty of jewelry for M'am and never lets a chance
> go by of paying her a compliment as if he thinks she's very beautiful.
> M'am doesn't listen to him. (de Jager 172-73)

Such a transposition of gendered selves reinforces even further the notion that Beyala's mission in this first novel of the series is more than to chronicle the *Bildungsprozess* of Loukoum. Beyala situates M'am's individuation all the more in the foreground as the narrative unfolds. Cazenave continues:

> When Loukoum feels bewildered, he grabs hold of woman in search of a little warmth. He needs contact and M'am's embraces. With each new expression, man betrays the depth of his pain and his vulnerability as a nonbeing, as the eternal immigrant. The image of the strong, domineering man who masters woman has disappeared . . . .Man has actually adopted the language of the victim, a language typically associated with woman. . . . Woman's value and image evolve from the rescuer and comforter to the person who disturbs the status quo through her own transformations. (*Rebellious Women* . . . 174-75)

Beyala re-inscribes traditional stereotypes and M'am breaks free from patriarchal constraint just enough to explore her burgeoning selfhood.

M'am is undoubtedly the more notably dynamic character in the text even though at times she appears to be the weakest and most marginalized one. Furthermore, her dynamism manifests itself overtly, as well. Patricia-Pia Celerier suggests that "[t]he survival of the kinship group is insured by the women who mostly, if sometimes subvertly, make the decisions. M'am sets up a jewelry business and comes to being able to offer the family its first vacation" (86). In the beginning, the bracelet business serves to supplement the family income since Abdou has been thrown in jail for false reporting of dependents for France's generous *allocations familiales*—government subsidies for families with children. M'am portrays self-reliance stepping in, directing and expanding her son's fledging business to provide financially for the family during difficult times. Likewise, she involves herself in tasks that necessitate artistry and a good deal of self-expression which contributes to her overall *Bildung*. Additionally, as Celerier cites, the family is able to afford a nice vacation (episodes recounted in *Maman*) to escape the frenzy of Paris because of M'am's profits (86). The vacation and ensuing adulterous relationship between M'am and Monsieur Tichit are the catalyzing moments in the second novel in the series. Thus, M'am's entrepreneurship is but another step in her development and awakening.

The search for unambiguous and authentic selfhood nevertheless remains problematic. Such mind over matter attitudes M'am exhibits as she sings and smiles through the difficulties of her daily routine cannot however completely overcome the complexities wrought by racial, gender and class biases. As Maria Umeh aptly asserts, "the African woman is caught in a terrible bind. In order to be free and fulfilled as a woman she must renounce her African identity because of the inherent sexism of traditional African culture. Or if she wishes to cherish and affirm her 'Africanness,' she must renounce her claims to feminine independence and self-determination" ("A Comparative Study . . . " 36). M'am finds herself in such a predicament. Yet what Rosowski and Felski theorize in general ways, readers see beginning to take shape specifically in this text. M'am awakens to her own personal development possibilities, yet she also becomes aware of insurmountable limitations to individuation.

Notes

1 This is from an interview with Beyala conducted by Narcisse Kombi.

2 On the back cover of the novel, the publisher, Albin Michel, states: "With a candor and a sense of humor that reminds one of *Le Petit Nicolas*, with Zazie's crudeness and cheekiness, Calixthe Beyala's *Petit Prince* gives us a gay and merry chronicle of life in Belleville. Blending laughter and emotion, a colorful community speaks as a whole, caught between the need for integration and the necessity to retain its roots." (translated from French)

3 Fanon's theories of racism and colonial domination are elaborated in *Peau Noire, Masques Blancs*, 1952.

4 Felski asserts that the moment of awakening is ahistorical or outside of history. It is a "self-enclosed moment" which "marks a threshold; it is a circumscribed moment, a point between two states, and cannot in itself generate any sequential process" (Felski 141). It is a "process of self-recognition rather than one of development" (Felski 141).

5 A thorough discussion of Ellis's ideas can be found in the Introduction and Chapter One of this book as well as in her book *Appearing to Diminish*. Lewisburg, PA: Bucknell UP, 1999.

Chapter 6

A Journey Ignites Awakening: Beyala's *Maman a un amant*

> *"Women's freedom generates bad seed. It grows any and everywhere, even between their thighs.*
> *It's not me who said this, it's my dad.*
> *And the first thing that I can assure you, is that M'am has A LOVER.*[1]*"*

Thus continues Loukoum's story in the second novel of the Belleville series. Written in 1993, just one year after *Le petit prince de Belleville*, *Maman a un amant* follows the Traoré family on its first vacation, its first foray outside the immigrant neighborhood in Paris. Once again, Loukoum, the little boy who guided readers through the events comprising Beyala's first Belleville installment, returns, this time 12 years old, to resume his family's story. Beyala retains much of the same feel to her story as Loukoum's tone, diction, and style as principal narrator remain largely unchanged. She again alternates Loukoum's

111

storyline with the philosophical musings of another. This time, however, instead of his father's perspectives on male victimization and female liberation within the context of post-colonial immigration; it is Loukoum's adopted mother M'am who imparts her viewpoints on female development and awakening and their attendant hardships.

Beyala relates up front that M'am's words appear as translated from the Bambara by Loukoum. It is most likely M'am's illiteracy in this instance (she does actively seek opportunities to learn to read and write later in the novel) rather than any sort of attempt by masculine powers to impede her right to speak her mind freely which necessitates translation of her thoughts by her son. However, given the often subtle yet plentiful occurrences of male-oriented hegemony dominating most societies, the latter possibility should never be completely eliminated. M'am's contributions to the overall story presented at the beginnings of each chapter offer direct insights into the psyche of a protagonist who faces the multiple jeopardies Deborah King and others have so poignantly described[2]. It is M'am's personal situation, she is a black, female African who lives in an immigrant neighborhood, to which readers become privy. Cazenave points out that "[u]nlike Abdou, she [M'am] does not extrapolate or draw conclusions about the African woman's general situation and status. . . . We knew her emotional state in [*Le petit prince de Belleville*], but here it is cast in a new light, presented from the perspective of the dominated person" (*Rebellious Women . . .* 208). Here again, because this is a deeply personal account offered by an individual focusing solely on her own circumstances, we know immediately that the remarks constitute autobiography and autobiography, as discussed earlier, remains the preferred form of novels of development and awakening. M'am's narrative chronicles various significant periods of her existence. Cazenave believes that "each of M'am's interventions constitutes a stage in her life: how she met Abdou, why she decided to follow him, her ensuing disappointment regarding France, her suffering from being barren, and the deterioration of their relationship. . . . She then recounts her changes in spirit, her lack of feelings for Abdou, and in the end her emptiness" (*Rebellious Women . . .* 208). Thus one is able to clearly trace M'am's development and awakening and how she arrives at her oft-repeated deduction given such a difficult existence: "Woman is born kneeling at man's feet" (Beyala, *Maman . . .* 21).

In her first proclamations, M'am conveys in general terms her views regarding how the world operates and her early despondency regarding personal escape. The quotation cited above is but one of such perspectives. Others follow parallel trains of thought: "I am reduced to indifference or to my least common denominator" (Beyala, *Maman . . .* 5) and "The equality of the sexes belongs to the domain of the abstract" (Beyala, *Maman . . .* 22) as well as "What could I do, friend? Rebel? In this postulate, no recovery is possible. The secret of remission? Pardon? What pardon? Burdensome mistake it is to be a woman. So burdensome that no punishment, even repentance on grievous, bended knee, might erase" (Beyala, *Maman . . .* 37). The oppressive conditions and heavy burdens of being a woman alluded to in *Le petit prince de Belleville* now find, in the words of Cazenave, "pragmatic and to the point" articulation in *Maman a un amant.* (*Rebellious Women* . . . 208). Yet such pointed commentary also divulges a changing spirit, one which acquiesces to growth and re-newed understanding. Facing all she does, M'am finds the hope to express, relatively early in her narrative, the following sentiment which guides her daily attitude. "Nevertheless, child, I have a feeling that no prison exists which is not a temple opening out onto a prairie" (Beyala, *Maman* . . . 38). From this ideological stance M'am continues to relate her emotionally charged story addressed, in a similar way to that of her husband, to her nameless Friend (l'Amie). A metaphorical prairie does indeed await her. In a different way, the larger story which Loukoum narrates, offers concrete and overt evidence of M'am's inner change in spirit.

At the close of *Le petit prince de Belleville*, M'am's entrepreneurship and independent spirit begins to show. While Abdou is incarcerated, she helps out with Loukoum's bracelet business in order to earn critical money for the household. She becomes so good at her work that she embarks on directing the business herself. Such burgeoning initiative later proves essential in M'am's development. As Beyala's sequel begins, Loukoum's recounting of the impact the news of M'am's lover makes in the community is followed closely by the story of how the family's vacation trip to Pompidou comes about and how Monsieur Tichit enters the picture. Loukoum recounts, albeit in a rather biased fashion, how the shocking events unfold:

> It's necessary to understand and pardon when one is able. That's true. One could not even count to a thousand before a married Muslim woman give herself over to public display. And how! This is the kind of news that makes one run around without knowing your mouth from your rear end.
> But things didn't happen all at once, like natural catastrophes on which you can't count.
> First, we had to go on vacation. (Beyala, *Maman* . . . 7)

The family's first excursion outside Paris proves to be an enlightening and exciting one for all. Loukoum notes that having enough money to spend time in the sun is not promised to anyone. But he adds "we were no longer your average Negroes. We had climbed the ladder. . . . We were dressed chez Tati, and hand-me-downs, we threw those in the city dump" (Beyala, *Maman* . . . 7). While these constitute the perspectives of a 12 year old and as such are somewhat embellished, with M'am's business and Abdou's more relaxed demeanor life is now much better for this family than it had ever been. When the rest of the community learns of the family's trip to Cannes (it is later revealed that the family is actually going to the village of Pompidou instead) and that M'am is paying for it, they are quite impressed. In fact, the news prompts Monsieur Kaba, one of the regulars at Monsieur Guillaume's café, to express his thoughts on the situation. The conversation unfolds in this manner:

> Monsieur Guillaume was quiet for a moment, then he said:
>   The Abdous are taking off to Cannes.
>   What!!! shrieked the Negroes in concert.
>   M'am is paying for a vacation to Cannes.
>   Not possible! I won't come back to it.
>   I told you so, said my Uncle Kaba holding up his middle finger un-
> der Monsieur Guillaume's nose. I swore to you that this woman
> would go far to watch out for her man all day long. Not like these . . .
> these . . . [prostitutes]. (Beyala, *Maman* . . . 14)

Most of the crowd at the café remains in disbelief of the family's plans, but Kaba has always sensed a different spirit in M'am, one that would bring her to pay for such a getaway and one that rouses her awakening and general growth as an individual.

In her study on the novel of self-discovery, Rita Felski contends that development of self-identity in novels about women is often triggered by some process of separation (135). Such was the case with Emecheta's Adah, she left her husband and went to live in what might be termed a female community in subsidized housing, and with Dangarembga's Tambu, she left her immediate family and went to the mission school and later on to Sacred Heart School, and such is the case in a sense with Beyala's M'am. Although M'am never divorces Abdou and at the end of *Maman*, they are living together as happily, at least on the surface, as ever, M'am does find herself benefiting from moments of separation from Abdou. As has been considered, the period of Abdou's imprisonment in *Le petit prince* is one of the first times the couple is apart and it is during this separation that M'am exhibits her budding independence with the bracelet business. While this is a temporary and short separation, its importance for future moments apart cannot be underestimated.

A large part of the action in *Maman* occurs outside of Belleville. Yet Loukoum reminds us that "This was the first time that we've gotten out of Paris seeing that getting paid enough to lay around in the sun is not a given for everyone" (Beyala, *Maman* . . . 7). If the family's excursion to the south is read as a separation writ large then, although M'am is never really physically distant from her family during the trip, she parts from interactions with fellow immigrants and thus their scrutiny and judgement. In addition, she separates herself as well from the drudgery of daily chores and routines and ultimately she detaches herself from her husband when she begins seeing Monsieur Tichit as a lover. Departure from Belleville serves to free M'am, if only temporarily, from many limiting factors in her life such as community interaction and domestic and family responsibilities. Additionally, the ability she has to front the money which accesses her path to awakening reveals the extent of her agency.

A Forbidden Relationship

"Mr. Tichit was smiling with pleasure. In an instant, the strap on M'um's dress slid, we almost saw the tips of her breasts. But that didn't disturb him. He said something in her ear. She smiled showing all of her teeth. Seeing her there, one couldn't imagine that she had family responsibilities.
Papa sat down under the veranda, continuously saying: «Damn Bitch!» repeatedly like that. As for me, things really weren't much better." Loukoum, describing the burgeoning relationship between M'am and Monsieur Tichit in *Maman a un amant*

M'am's relationship with Monsieur Tichit develops progressively. In fact, when Madame Trauchessec, owner of the house in Pompidou where everyone is staying, introduces the Traorés to Monsieur Tichit, a fellow lodger-to-be, the latter reacts strongly against another family staying there. Monsieur Tichit and his daughter Goélène want peace and quiet so that he can rest and recuperate from heart trouble. The Traoré family's cool welcome warms rather quickly especially when Tichit takes notice of M'am's natural beauty and attractiveness. Loukoum recounts the flirtatious comments Tichit directs at M'am: "He continuously eyes M'am, to spin loving gestures: "Excuse me, Madame. —My sincerest respect, Madame. —Your beauty is equaled only by your charm" (Beyala, *Maman . . .* 76). Later as Tichit and M'am talk more, he inundates her with stories of his adventures and heroism and she is fascinated and drawn to him. Loukoum notes: "But he really has such passionate stories that each one caught our attention. M'am encourages him. She continuously lets out laughs that echo to the ceiling. . . . She encourages him. She asks loads of questions. And China? Are you familiar with China? I would like to go to China" (Beyala, *Maman . . .* 47). M'am's feelings change and she is awakened to new desires and sees fresh potential for herself. After M'am has lived a rather dull and tumultuous twenty two years as Abdou's wife, Tichit appears to be able to offer an alternative existence, one filled with exciting activity, respect and perhaps enough autonomy for her to be who she wants to be. Consequently, Tichit and M'am end up spending a lot time together.

Beyond his very public sweet talking, flattery and verbal exaltation of M'am, Tichit soon steers their conversation toward the sexual act. Soon after the family's arrival in Pompidou, Tichit opens the bathroom door one morning as M'am is completing her ablutions. According to Loukoum, "she meowed like a cat whose paws had just been stepped on. He excused himself but he stood there staring at M'am's breasts. One might say that he wanted to snatch up the sky" (Beyala, *Maman . . .* 77). Later that very day, Loukoum, while out for a walk, stumbles across M'am and Tichit sharing a quiet moment. As Loukoum listens in, Tichit pointedly turns the conversation toward M'am and Abdou's sexual practices:

>   You still love him? he asks her.
>   I don't know. I am still slightly passionate for him. It's true that if I
> took the notion to take a husband, it would be him. But he's so weak.
> He doesn't know what he wants. Sometimes he slaps me. He has
> things that I like and lots that I don't like.
>   You like sleeping with him?
>   No. He knows it too. What does it do for me, huh? He gets on top
> of me, sticks his thing inside. As for me, it's like I'm not even there.
> He does his little thing, flops over and goes to sleep.
>   Does his little thing? but Maryam, one would think he uses you for
> his urinal!
>   In any case, that's how I see things . . .
>   You never felt anything? he asks.
>   Almost nothing.
>   So then you are a virgin?
>   Me?
>   Listen Maryam. Inside your organ, there's a little button which tin-
> gles nicely when you do it with someone.
>   You mean when you have sex?
>   That's right. It gets warmer and warmer and becomes moist. It's
> really very nice. (Beyala, *Maman* . . . 78)

For M'am the notion that she too can derive pleasure from sexual intercourse is
remarkable. More and more, M'am's thoughts and conceptions of the world
around her are liberated. Slowly, she awakens to re-newed possibility. Interestingly Beyala orchestrates this stage of M'am's awakening, narrated by
Loukoum, to coincide with one of her more negative commentaries on her life
with Abdou which opens the same chapter. M'am reflects:

>   During these years, I tried to be a good wife.
>   I celebrated my husband as the other mystery of life, I repeated gal-
> axies of stars over his body and when it was time the mark of the
> heavens. I whispered unheard of sweet nothings in his ears.
>   I was his, banished from the world, separated from the light . . .
>   We lived together, but I was all alone . . .
>   I was dying of sadness.
>   I was dying of shame.
>   I no longer knew how to bow down to pray.
>   What did it matter? Who would listen to me? Who would wash
> away the heresy? The sin? (Beyala, *Maman* . . . 74-5)

Tichit appears to offer M'am an alternative to the life she describes having led
with Abdou above. M'am believes herself to be on a path to renewed understanding as, on the surface at least, all appears to be opening afresh for her. Life
seems new and different, she no longer feels "banished from the world, separated from the light" (Beyala, *Maman* . . . 74).
      While Tichit woos her with seemingly sincere, yet trite expressions of his
undying love and offers advice for more enjoyable lovemaking, it becomes ap-

parent all too quickly that his sexual advances toward M'am derive from his own lust. Loukoum, with childlike keenness, sees clearly through his advances: "This Mr. Tichit has the skills of those people who make lies seem more true than reality itself" (Beyala, *Maman*. . . 47). Cazenave, likewise, suggests that M'am is again being used by a man. She writes: "The man who seemed to love her, who would show her another way of life, was thinking only of his own satisfaction and sexual pleasure. Mr. Tichit's selfishness proves every bit as strong as Abdou's" (*Rebellious Women* . . . 187). Indeed, Tichit's name could be read "Petit Shit" = "P'tit shit" = "Tichit." Such a reading then aptly describes the man's behavior and attitude toward M'am while reinforcing universal patriarchal dominance. Nevertheless, because M'am allows herself to savor novel experiences with a man who, on the surface at least, appears to be the opposite of her husband, it takes her a while to realize Tichit's egotism. Tichit appears at first to offer M'am an appreciation and a freedom she has never really felt with Abdou, but in the end, he too comes up short. In the final analysis, Beyala communicates once more the characteristic denunciation of patriarchal power structures for which her works are known. In M'am's case, as will soon be demonstrated, Tichit is another treacherous curve on her path to re-newed understanding.

At least twice, M'am is caught being intimate with Monsieur Tichit. Despite his self-centered motives, M'am rebels and gives in to sexual exploration with Tichit. While they are still on vacation, the police are called in to help look for her and soon they discover that she is in Tichit's room. After pressuring Abdou to press charges against her and divorce her, the police leave Abdou to his own recourse. Abdou does not follow through with anything. Instead, he and M'am go to their bed and awaken the next morning is if nothing has happened. They also tell the kids that nothing really happened even though they know that Loukoum knows all. M'am reminds Loukoum that "there are things that should not be repeated to anyone. To anyone, you understand? As for the Whites, dirty laundry is washed within the family. We can do the same and save appearances. You understand? (Beyala, *Maman* . . . 117-18). The family returns to Paris this day and for a while things appear normal.

Back in Paris, M'am, on Tichit's prompting, decides that she will go to school and learn to read and to write. Such skills would open doors for her and allow her to become more independent. M'am's experiences during their vacation have brought her to the awareness that educational opportunities such as literacy courses would facilitate individuation and development. She shares her thoughts:

> Oh, Friend, I have not renounced my lover . . . He is above and be-
> yond the warm breath of an embrace, he reinvents me . . .
>   He says: "You must learn to read and to write."
>   That's a thought which scares me . . .

> I want to go to the end of this experience, there discover pleasures
> so that I will never have to submit myself again to the remorse of my
> abandoned desert.
> I am learning to read and to write, and this passion, so newly born,
> teaches me how better to account for rhythm and passion.
> I am learning how to designate things by words, signs. I spell them
> one by one to tame them . . .
> I lose their definitions, their connotations, but their smells stay with
> me all day long. This is a difficult path to access, especially when
> you consider, Friend, that I have spent half a century walled in by ig-
> norance. (Beyala, *Maman* . . . 208-09)

Not surprisingly, when M'am shares her news, Abdou is again outdone and he grills her: "What do you want really? To kill me? To render the kids orphans?...Where're you goin' with all this? Becoming an intellectual? For what, huh? There's no work for you. No one could hire you. You're black, you're old, don't forget it. No one would take you, even as a prostitute" (Beyala, *Maman* . . . 145). Nevertheless, M'am perseveres and with some encouragment from Aminata, Loukoum's biological mother and a well-to-do prostitute, she goes to school to learn to read and to write. Aminata proclaims: "So, the devil with Abdou. And go learn to read and to write if that rings your bell" (Beyala, *Maman* . . . 149). Beyala uses a prostitute, and not just any prostitute, but the biological mother of her adopted son, as a mouthpiece for truth and encouragement in M'am's *Bildungsprozess*. Beyala continues to subvert traditional paradigms of power and agency.

Out for a walk one day, Loukoum spots M'am sitting in a café accompanied by another man. He quickly realizes that it is Tichit: "I thought this fellow was still in Pompidou enjoying himself silly in the sun, the streams, and the mountains. He really was in Belleville" (Beyala, *Maman* . . . 129-30). He overhears some of their conversation in which Tichit tells M'am that she has the right to be with him if she wants, to love him, and to neglect her other responsibilities despite what others in the community might say. And seeing that she never really has been happy with Abdou and their relationship is more like that of two siblings than two lovers, it would make more sense if she followed her heart and committed to him. Tichit, trying to convince her, asserts: "Hold your horses! People have other things to do than take care of business that has nothing to do with them. We live in a world where everyone is looking for himself: ants, bees, functionaries, and even married women" (Beyala, *Maman* . . . 130). Yet here M'am's reluctance to move forward with this illegitimate relationship because of an overwhelming sense of duty, responsibility, and concern for what the rest of the African community would think of her evinces itself. A return from the freeing countryside to familiar Belleville triggers in her a return to Abdou and maternal duties. Although M'am feels that her relationship with Tichit is morally wrong, they continue to see each other when they can. Angry that M'am "[wants to be like all of the women [in France], Abdou falls apart emotionally and eventually refuses to let M'am come home (Beyala, *Maman* . . . 205). Men from Monsieur Guillaume's café check in on him and Aminata cooks and cleans up after Loukoum and the other children. In the end, Tichit's reminders of all they had together are not enough to convince M'am to stay with him. M'am's moral responsibility to her family triumphs and she decides to leave Tichit for good.

Conclusion

> "*I came back, Friend.*
> *I remain mute in front of this simple portrait of a man . . .*
> *How much I want to say, have the right to say again, this half a century of reclusion!*
> *How much I want to scream for lost love on the wing of a bird, dying in the sun!*
> *I remain mute.*
> *Moored in this smelly port, this reassuring but dull haven.*
> *I will not tell him that in the arms of my lover, I was introduced to brilliant flowering fields, where pure souls entwined.*"
> M'am, *Maman a un amant*

M'am comes home. Indeed she returns to her husband, to her children, and to her domestic responsibilities. While a whole host of friends and neighbors are there to greet her, it is grand-mère Balbine, "the most decrepit one in France," according to Loukoum, who speaks (Beyala, *Maman . . .* 243). Sharing the glaringly chauvinistic folk legend of how man and woman first became a couple, grand-mère Balbine reminds M'am that she is to be "the light of this home" (Beyala, *Maman . . .* 244). Balbine continues: "You are life. Whatever suffering your husband puts you through, you musn't lower yourself by imitating him. You must remain worthy. Never forget: You are the superior spirit who guides man" (Beyala, *Maman . . .* 244-45). Grand-mère Balbine's words of advice appear almost impossible to reconcile with the realities of modern life for women like M'am. Additionally, notes Cazenave, the legend "confirms man's traditional domination" of woman and empowers the community to police its individual constituents. "In reality," asserts Cazenave, "the community's final exhultation sanctions the woman's docility and the reestablishment of the hierarchical, patriarchal order (*Rebellious Women . . .* 188). However, our discussion here revolves around the re-awakening to authentic self-hood, that "recovery of a repressed identity and a consequent refusal of social and communal responsibilities which do not accord with internal desires" (Felski 135). Does M'am experience such an awakening? The answer is undeniably Yes, but it must be added that M'am's awakening leads only to a temporary taste of what full self-individuation and sexual liberation might be like.

Even though the reader holds high hopes throughout both novels for the continued progression of M'am's self-discovery; in the end, permanent liberation remains illusive. Onyeoziri observes that "à la fin du *Petit prince de Belleville*, nous constatons l'émergence d'une 'nouvelle femme' qui réclame son droit à la parole, à l'indépendence économique et au plaisir sexuel, nous promettant un rapport plus équilibré entre les deux sexes. Toutefois, la suite (Maman a un amant) est moins optimiste" (7-8) ["at the end of *The Little Prince of Belleville*, we witness the emergence of a "new woman" who reclaims her freedom to speak, to financial independence, and to sexual pleasure, promising us a more balanced relationship between the sexes. However, the sequel (*Maman a un amant*) is less optimistic]. In *Maman a un amant*, M'am gains her own voice and speaking for herself, but through Loukoum as interpreter, she recounts the various stages of her life. Her themes are as diverse as her life has been eventful: how life was with Abdou, what she felt she was missing, her desire to be with her lover and her fleeting taste of sexual liberation, her yearning to read and to write, and ultimately her desire to take care of her family once again. M'am is able to accomplish so much with so little and so quietly. From the family vacation, to times with her lover and to opening her mind through reading and writing for herself, M'am is indeed roused to re-newed understanding of how her life might be one day. Yet, as we know, she is hastily drawn back to the home, to responsibility and the community because the community itself refuses to set her free. Despite motivational challenges to M'am to be the light of her home and the fact that Abdou now has a job, Celerier acknowledges that at the end of *Maman*, "very little has changed" (90). Beyala's indictment of patriarchy in these texts points out the difficulties a woman faces as a *Bildungsheld*. Despite struggles, clear *Bildung* progress is made in these novels. M'am awakens to the possibility of a better life even though immediate access to such a life is stalled.

Beyala insists she concerns herself primarily with the status of the individual[3] and even though her narrator would suggest otherwise, it is her depiction of the struggle of the individual to define herself in relation to the community which pulses wildly through her works. Throughout both novels, *Le petit prince de Belleville* and *Maman a un amant*, the words "Solidarité oblige" echo loudly and Loukoum closes the latter by reminding us where ultimate authority apparently resides: "The spirit of the tribe is all that counts" (Beyala, *Maman* . . . 246). Felski notes that in novels of self-discovery and awakening "the question of how personal female identity is to be adequately integrated into a new social identity is often left unanswered" (136) and her counterpart Rosowski would remind us that for women, the process of awakening is most often "an awakening to limitations" (49). Beyala, however, continues to expose, identify, and chisel away at the prevalent and seemingly insurmountable patriarchal and postcolonial powers, those in the West and beyond, that continuously compel her female characters to compromise enduring states of authentic selfhood. Certainly, as a prolific and often controversial Cameroonian writer living in Paris who remains in touch with her culture and tradition, Beyala has set herself on the correct path for helping women like M'am gain access to personal *Bildung*. Beyala shares the story of an oppressed soul who eventually realizes that her life can be more fulilled in certain ways. Like traditional *Bildung* protagonists,

M'am undergoes a process of growth and maturation. For her, though, ultimate and authentic selfhood is still a ways off. One day, we remain hopeful that she will not only be able to see the prairie on the horizon just beyond the prison window, but reach it as well.

Notes

1 All translations from the French for *Maman a un amant* are those of the author of this book.
2 In King's conception, black women face multiple jeopardy—because of the three interdependent control systems of racism, sexism, and classism—in day to day living. For more, see King, Deborah K. "Multiple Jeopardy, Multiple Consciousness: The Context of a Black Feminist Ideology." *Signs* 14 (1988): 42-72.
3 See interview with Beyala conducted by Françoise Cévaër for further details.

Conclusion

What Lies Down the Path?

> "*The forms that it [the Bildungsroman] may assume in adapting itself to an even more complex world than ours, are infinite, and pass beyond our conjecture. But we can safely predict for it an even more rich and varied life than it has lived between Goethe's time and our own.*" Susanne Howe, 1930

> "*There is no cheap or easy pathway . . . to the brave new world of female equality and integrity. In fact, the road to individual strength is very private, often difficult and lonely.*" Lloyd W. Brown, 1981

African feminism has been shown, here in this study and elsewhere, to have notably different characteristics as well as motives when compared to mainstream white Western Feminism. In addition, it is evident that the application of the Western expression of Feminism proves futile for yielding insightful interpretations of African literature. However, it appears that the use of some theoretical foundations, like expansions of those associated with the traditional *Bildungsroman*, can generate enlightening results. With the application of novel of development theories and concepts in the spirit of Howe and Kontje, African literary texts, like those examined in this study, become fresh new frontiers for *Bildung* exploration.

Emecheta's *Second-Class Citizen* and *In the Ditch*, Dangarembga's *Nervous Conditions*, as well as Beyala's *Le petit prince de Belleville* and *Maman a un amant* recount the stories of women who, to varying degrees and by different means, find qualified escape and expand toward individuation. In all cases, the women have undergone a migrational shift made possible, for better or for worse, by European colonization of Nigeria, Cameroon, and Rhodesia (now Zimbabwe). With Emecheta, Adah finds herself with her family on what was to be a temporary stay in London for university study, with Dangarembga, Tambu moves from outside the relative constancy and stability of the traditional Rhodesian familial compound first to a mission school run by her "been to" uncle and aunt and later to the Sacred Heart School, and with Beyala, an entire family relocates permanently to France to set up their lives in an immigrant quarter of the capital city. Such movement activates for the women in the novels desires to grow, to become educated, to experience fully their surroundings and to enlighten the darker corners of their lives through personal development. Even with so much opportunity, life is never easy. What the West offers formerly colonized individuals, even within a post-independence context, is offered in such a way as to constitute a kind of neo-colonization or a re-colonization of already beleaguered individuals. Thus the official goal of the majority of nineteenth-century European colonial efforts, that of bringing "civilization" and "knowledge" to "backward and savage heathens," resurrects itself. The possibility of such inauthentic transformations lurks subtly in most every post-colonial novel of development, but an author's personal experiences and the path on which she guides female characters and where she ultimately leaves them must receive priority consideration. Emecheta, Dangarembga and Beyala reside and make their living in the West and opportunity there has been remarkable for each of them. Yet it is absolutely clear from their corpora of texts that they are not Westerners. They retain African sensibilities, storytelling patterns and vital cultural connections to their respective native countries. Similarly, the authors' female protagonists all lead lives which have been influenced, either directly or indirectly, by Western ways; yet elements of their native cultures continue to prove most valuable as they forge paths toward self-development.

Although Adah, Tambu and M'am have been removed from their familiar spaces, however wholesome, nurturing, and stable they may have been, new horizons and possibilities present themselves and they are clever enough to benefit from such prospects while guarding themselves from most of the pitfalls such opportunities bring. Howe perhaps put it best: "no one can learn much of anything at home. Going somewhere is the thing. And there—in all sorts of tempting variety—is [the] story" (1). These heroines' movements outside their native comfort zones, however, are not simply happy-go-lucky adventures as obstacles arise on multiple levels. As examined in this book in Chapters Two through Six, Adah, Tambu (as well as "the four women whom [she] loved"), and

M'am face conflicted and tortuous paths to expansion and re-newed understanding. In their development, the women encounter and deal with complications ranging from meddlesome parents-in-law to unrelenting spousal abuse and sibling rivalry, to age old sexism, racism, and classism and community pressure to shape up and act like a good woman should. By the end of each text, but not by far the end of these characters' stories, the female *Bildungshelde* have indeed grown and developed in qualified ways even if their respective situations promise further personal challenges. Like their authors, they have remained closely connected to their native culture as their authentic selfhood developed.

As long as networks of patriarchal and imperial power structures and ideologies remain, female characters such as the ones discussed here and real women—like the three authors of these novels or anyone else—find demonstrating agency and subjectivity deeply challenging. It should be noted as well that even the women in the works who have had complete access to excellent educational opportunities like Dangarembga's Maiguru and Nyasha and the ones who have wholly adopted so-called sexually liberating lifestyles like Beyala's Aminata find no feasible short cut in the process of *Bildung* as different challenges confront them. Indeed, "[t]here is no cheap or easy pathway . . . to the brave new world of female equality and integrity. In fact, the road to individual strength is very private, often difficult and lonely" (Brown 182). Brown's summation accurately portrays these women's struggles. Nevertheless, recording the events of one's own story, in whatsoever veiled terms they might be told, as Emecheta, Dangarembga and Beyala have set forth can be seen as a first step toward individual expansion. After all, "autobiographical writing," as cited in Chapter Two, "[is] regarded as a language to articulate self-definition" (Sougou 32). The burning of her first attempt at such writing is finally what drives Adah away from her husband who has treated her so badly and sets her up for further stages in her *Bildungsprozess*. While Adah's autobiography takes the shape of a real manuscript she writes and shows others, Tambu and M'am's "autobiographies" are presented by Dangarembga and Beyala respectively as a moving story recounted at a temporal distance to an audience by Tambu, who becomes in essence the "author" of the text and as the intimate thoughts and philosophical musings of woman who wants to enjoy not only her family but her own sexual longings. The routes toward self-definition underway in these texts are multiple as the *Bildungsprozess* of both author and character(s) of a given work simultaneously take shape. The novelists and the novels celebrate high hopes for brighter horizons for all women with the understanding that full potential for authentic individuation lies down the path.

Bibliography

Primary Sources

Beyala, Calixthe. *Le petit prince de Belleville*. Paris: Albin Michel, 1992.
————. *Maman a un amant*. Paris: Albin Michel, 1993.
Dangarembga, Tsitsi. *Nervous Conditions*. Seattle: Seal Press, 1988.
Emecheta, Buchi. *In the Ditch*. Oxford and Portsmouth, NH: Heinemann, 1972.
————. *Second Class Citizen*. New York: George Braziller, 1974.
de Jager, Marjolijn., trans. *Loukoum, the Little Prince of Belleville*. By Calixthe Beyala. Oxford and Portsmouth, NH: Heinemann, 1995.

Secondary Sources

Abel, Elizabeth, Marianne Hirsch, and Elizabeth Langland. *The Voyage In: Fictions of Female Development*. Hanover and London: University Press of New England, 1983.
Achebe, Chinua. *Morning Yet on Creation Day*. Garden City: Anchor, Doubleday, 1976.
Aegerter, Lindsay Pentolfe. "A Dialectic of Autonomy and Community: Tsitsi Dangarembga's *Nervous Conditions*." *Tulsa Studies in Women's Literature* 15.1 (1996): 231-40.
Amrine, Frederick. "Rethinking the '*Bildungsroman*.'" *Michigan Germanic Studies* 13.2 (1987): 119-39.

Andrade, Susan. "Rewriting History, Motherhood, and Rebellion: Naming an African Women's Literary Tradition." *Research in African Literatures* 21.2 (1990): 91-110.

Androne, Mary Jane. "Tsitsi Dangarembga's *Nervous Conditions*: An African Woman's Revisionist Narrative." *Ngũgĩ Wa Thiong'o, Texts and Contexts*. Ed. Charles Cantaluop. Trenton, NJ: African World Press, 1995. 323-32.

Arndt, Susan. *The Dynamics of African Feminism. Defining and Classifying the African Feminist Literatures*. Trans. Isabel Cole. Trenton, NJ: Africa World Press, 2002.

Ashcroft, Bill, Gareth Griffiths, and Helen Tiffin. *The Empire Writes Back*. London and New York: Routledge, 1989.

————. *The Post-Colonial Studies Reader*. London and New York: Routledge, 1995.

Beauvoir, Simone de. *Le deuxième sexe*. 2 vols. Paris: Gallimard, 1949.

Begum, Khani. "Construction of the Female Subject in Postcolonial Literature: Tsitsi Dangarembga's *Nervous Conditions*." *Journal of Commonwealth and Postcolonial Studies* 1.1 (1993): 21-27.

Berghahn, Klaus L. "From Classicist to Classical Literary Criticism, 1730-1806." *A History of German Literary Criticism, 1730-1980*. Ed. Peter Uwe Hohendahl. Lincoln: University of Nebraska Press, 1988. 13-98.

Beyala, Calixthe. Online Interview conducted by Narcisse Mouellé Kombi. AMINA. Aug. 1992. 19 Jan. 1999.<www.arts.uwa.edu.au/AFLIT/AMINA Beyala 1992.html>.

Birch, Eva Lennox. "Autobiography: The Art of Self-Definition." *Black Women's Writing*. Ed. Gina Wisker. New York: St. Martin's Press, 1993. 127-45.

Blackwell, Jeannine. "Bildungsroman mit Dame: The Heroine in the German Bildungsroman from 1770 to 1900." Diss. Indiana University, 1982.

Brench, A. C. *The Novelists' Inheritance in French Africa: Writers from Senegal to Cameroon*. London: Oxford University Press, 1967.

Buckley, Jerome H. *Season of Youth: the Bildungsroman from Dickens to Golding*. Cambridge: Harvard University Press, 1974.

Buma, Pascal Pensena. "The Bildungsroman and Selfhood: Beyond Race, Gender, and Culture." Diss. Pennsylvania State University, 1997.

Casenave, Odile. "Calixthe Beyala: l'exemple d'une écriture décentrée dans le roman africain au féminin." *L'écriture décentrée*. Ed. Michel Laronde. Paris: L'Harmattan, 1996. 123-47.

————. *Rebellious Women. The New Generation of Female African Novelists*. Boulder, CO: Lynne Rienner, 2000.

Celerier, Patricia-Pia. "'The Disorder of Order': Constructions of Masculinity in the Works of Mongo Beti and Calixthe Beyala." *Romance Notes* 36 (1995): 83-92.

Cévaër, Françoise. "Interview de Calixthe Beyala (Romancière Camerounaise)." *Revue de Littérature Comparée* 1 (1993): 161-64.

Chemain-Degrange, Arlette. *Emancipation féminine et roman africain*. Dakar: Nouvelles Editions Africaines, 1980.

Chukukere, Gloria Chineze. *Gender Voices and Choices : Redefining Women in Contemporary African Fiction*. Enugu, Nigeria: Fourth Dimension Publishing, 1995.

Cocalis, Susan L. "The Transformation of *Bildung* from an Image to an Ideal." *Monatshefte* 70.4 (1978): 399-414.

Corngold, Stanley. *The Fate of the Self : German Writers and French Theory*. New York: Columbia University Press, 1986.

Davis, Christina. "Mother and Writer: Means of Empowerment in the Work of Buchi Emecheta." *Commonwealth* 13.1 (1990): 13-21.

Durand, Alain-Philippe. "Le côté de Belleville: Négociation de l'espace migratoire chez Calixthe Beyala." *Études Francophones*. 14.2 (1999): 53-65.

Ellis, Lorna. *Appearing to Diminish: Female Development and the British Bildungsroman, 1750-1850*. Lewisburg, PA: Bucknell University Press, 1999.

Emecheta, Buchi. "Feminism with a small 'f'!" *Criticism and Ideology: Second African Writers' Conference Stockholm 1986*. Ed. Kirsten Holst Petersen. Uppsala: Scandinavian Institute of African Studies, 1988.

Fanon, Frantz. *Les Damnés de la terre*. Paris: La Découverte, 1961.

————. *Peau noire, masques blancs*. Paris: Seuil, 1952.

Felski, Rita. "The Novel of Self-Discovery A Necessary Fiction?" *Southern Review* 19 (1986): 131-148.

Fishburn, Katherine. *Reading Buchi Emecheta: Cross-Cultural Conversations*. Contributions to the Study of World Literature 61. Westport, CT: Greenwood Press, 1995.

Flewellen, Elinor C. "Assertiveness vs. Submissiveness in Selected Works by African Women Writers." *Ba Shirui: A Journal of African Languages and Literatures*. 12.2 (1985): 3-18.

Foucault, Michel. *The History of Sexuality, Volume I: An Introduction*. Trans. Robert Hurley. New York: Vintage, 1990.

Friedman, Susan Stanford. "Women's Autobiographical Selves: Theory and Practice." *The Private Self: Theory and Practice of Women's Autobiographical Writings*. Ed. Shari Benstock. London: Routledge, 1988. 34-62.

Gairola, Rahul K. "Western Experiences: Education and 'Third World Women' in the Fictions of Tsitsi Dangarembga and Meena Alexander." *Jouvert: A Journal of Postcolonial Studies*. 4.2 (2000): 30 pars. 23 June 2003 <http://social.chass.ncsu.edu/jouvert/ index.htm>.

Gallimore, Rangira Béatrice. *L'Œuvre Romanesque de Calixthe Beyala*. Paris: L'Harmattan, 1997.

Gates, Henry Louis, Jr. ed. *"Race," Writing, and Difference*. Chicago and London: University of Chicago Press, 1986.

Hardin, James. *Reflection and Action: Essays on the Bildungsroman*. Columbia: University of South Carolina Press, 1991.

Hegel, G. W. F. *Phenomenology of Spirit.* Trans. A. V. Miller. Oxford: Oxford University Press, 1977.

Herd, E. W., and August Obermayer. eds. *A Glossary of German Literary Terms.* Otago German Studies 2. Dunedin, New Zealand: Department of German, 1992.

Howe, Susanne. *Wilhem Meister and his English Kinsmen: Apprentices to Life.* New York: Columbia University Press, 1930.

Internet Modern History Sourcebook. Ed. Paul Halsall. Aug. 1997. Fordham University. 4 Dec. 2003 <http://www.fordham.edu/halsall/mod/indrevtabs1.html>.

Jameson, Fredric. "Third-World Literature in the Era of Multinational Capitalism." *Social Text.* 15 (1986): 65-88.

Jules-Rosette, Bennetta. *Black Paris. The African Writers' Landscape.* Urbana and Chicago: University of Illinois Press, 1998.

Killam, G. D. *The Writings of Chinua Achebe.* London: Heinemann, 1977.

King, Deborah K. "Multiple Jeopardy, Multiple Consciousness: The Context of a Black Feminist Ideology." *Signs* 14 (1988): 42-72.

Kombi, Narcisse Mouellé. "Calixthe Beyala et son *Petit Prince de Belleville.*" Reprinted from *Amina* 268 (1992): 10-12.

Kontje, Todd. *The German Bildungsroman: History of a National Genre.* Columbia, SC: Camden House, 1993.

Labovitz, Esther K. *The Myth of the Heroine: The Female Bildungsroman in the Twentieth Century.* New York: Peter Lang, 1986.

Lange, Victor. ed. *Goethe: A Collection of Critical Essays.* Englewood Cliffs: Prentice-Hall, 1968.

———. "Goethe's Craft of Fiction." Lange 65-85.

LeSeur, Geta. *Ten is the Age of Darkness: The Black Bildungsroman.* Columbia: University of Missouri Press, 1995.

Lewis, Désirée. "Myths of Motherhood and Power: The Construction of 'Black Woman' in Literature." *English in Africa* 19.1 (1992): 35-51.

Lukács, Georg. *The Meaning of Contemporary Realism.* Trans. John Mander and Necker Mander. London: Merlin Press, 1963.

———. *The Theory of the Novel.* Trans. Anna Bostock. Cambridge, MA: MIT Press, 1971.

———. "Wilhelm Meisters Lehrjahre." Lange 86-98.

Mahoney, Dennis F. "The Apprenticeship of the Reader: The Bildungsroman of the 'Age of Goethe'." Hardin 97-117.

Mbom, Clément. "Nouvelles tendances de la création romanesque chez Calixthe Beyala." *Voix nouvelles du roman africain.* Eds. Daniel Delas and Danielle Deltel. Nanterre, France: Université Paris X, 1994. 49-72.

McWilliams, Sally. "Tsitsi Dangarembga's Nervous Conditions: At the Cross-roads of Feminism and Post-Colonialism.'" *World Literature Written in English.* 31.1 (1991): 103-112.

Miller, Christopher. *Theories of Africans. Francophone Literature and Anthropology in Africa.* Chicago: University of Chicago Press, 1990.

Mohanty, Chandra Talpade, Ann Russo, and Lourdes Torres. Eds. *Third World Women and the Politics of Feminism.* Bloomington: Indiana University Press, 1991.

Moretti, Franco. *The Way of the World: The Bildungsroman in European Culture.* London: Verso, 1987.

Newell. Stephanie. Ed. *Writing African Women. Gender, Popular Culture and Literature in West Africa.* London: Zed, 1997.

Nfah-Abbenyi, Juliana Makuchi. *Gender in African Women's Writing: Identity, Sexuality, and Difference.* Bloomington: Indiana University Press, 1997.

Ngcobo, Lauretta. "African Motherhood—Myth or Reality." *Criticism and Ideology.* Ed. Kristen Holst Petersen. Uppsala: Scandinavian Institute of African Studies, 1988. 141-54.

Nnaemeka, Obioma. Ed. *The Politics of (M)Othering. Womanhood, Identity, and Resistance in African Literature.* London: Routledge, 1997.

Ogundipe-Leslie, 'Molara. "Not Spinning on the Axis of Maleness." In *Sisterhood is Global. The International Women's Movement Anthology.* Ed. Robin Morgan. New York: Anchor, Doubleday, 1984. 498-504.

Onyeoziri, Gloria Nne. "Les petits princes de Beyala." *Études Francophones.* 16.2 (2002): 7-24.

Ojaide, Tanure, and Joseph Obi. *Culture, Society, and Politics in Modern African Literature.* Durham, NC: Carolina Academic Press, 2002.

Owomoyela, Oyekan. *African Literatures: An Introduction.* Waltham, MA: Crossroads Press, 1979.

Phillips, Maggi. "Engaging Dreams: Alternative Perspectives on Flora Nwapa, Buchi Emecheta, Ama Ata Aidoo, Bessie Head, and Tsitsi Dangarembga's Writing." *Research in African Literatures.* 25.1 (1994): 89-103.

Podis, Leonard A., and Yakubu Saaka. Eds. *Challenging Hierarchies. Issues and Themes in Colonial and Postcolonial African Literature.* New York: Peter Lang, 1998.

Porter, Abioseh Michael. "Second Class Citizen: The Point of Departure for Understanding Buchi Emecheta's Major Fiction." *The International Fiction Review.* 15.2 (1988): 123-29.

Reed, T. J. *The Classical Centre: Goethe and Weimar 1775-1832.* London: Croom Helm, 1980.

Rosello, Mireille. *Declining the Stereotype: Ethnicity and Representation in French Cultures.* Hanover, NH: University Press of New England (Dartmouth College), 1998.

———. "Du bon usage des stéréotypes orientalisants: vol et recel de préjugés anti-maghrébins dans les années 1990." *L'Esprit Créateur* 34 (1994): 42-57.

————. *Infiltrating Culture. Power and Identity in Contemporary Women's Writing*. Manchester, Eng.: Manchester University Press, 1996.

Rosowski, Susan J. "The Novel of Awakening." Abel, Hirsch, and Langland 49-68.

Sammons, Jeffrey L. "The Bildungsroman for Nonspecialists: An Attempt at a Clarification." Hardin 26-45.

————. "The Mystery of the *Bildungsroman*, or: What Happened to Wilhelm Meister's Legacy?" *Genre* 14 (1981): 229-246.

Sarr, Ndiawar. "The Female Protagonist as Part of a Transitional Generation in *The Joys of Motherhood*." *Bridges* 5.2 (1993): 25-33.

Shaffner, Randolph P. *The Apprenticeship Novel*. New York: Peter Lang, 1984.

Shumway, David. *Michel Foucault*. Charlottesville: University Press of Virginia, 1992.

Sougou, Omar. *Writing Across Cultures. Gender Politics and Difference in the Fiction of Buchi Emecheta*. Amsterdam: Rodopi, 2002.

Steinecke, Hartmut. *Romantheorie und Romankritik in Deutschland: Die Entwicklund des Gattungsverständnisses von der Scott-Rezeption bis zum programmatischen Realismus*. Vol. 1 Stuttgart: Metzler, 1975.

Stratton, Florence. "The Shallow Grave: Archetypes of Female Experience in African Fiction." *Research in African Literatures* 19.1 (1988): 143-69.

Strobel, Margaret. "Women's History, Gender History, and European Colonialism." *Colonialism and the Modern World*. Eds. Gregory Blue, Martin Bunton, and Ralph Croizier. Armonk, NY: M. E. Sharpe, 2002. 51-68.

Sugnet, Charles. "Nervous Conditions: Dangarembga's feminist reinvention of Fanon." Nnaemeka 33-49.

Thomas, R. Hinton. "The Uses of 'Bildung.'" *German Life and Letters*. 30 (1977): 177-186.

Torti, Carola, Karin Kilb, and Mark Stein. "*Groping for Coherence: Patriarchal Constraints and Female Resistance in Tsitsi Dangarembga's* Nervous Conditions." *Fusions of Culture*. 26 (1996): 247-254.

Umeh, Davidson, and Maria A. Umeh. "An Interview with Buchi Emecheta." *Ba Shiru*. 12.2 (1985): 19-25.

Umeh, Maria A. "A Comparative Study of the Idea of Motherhood in Two Third World Novels." *College Language Association Journal* 31.1 (1987): 31-43.

Uwakweh, Pauline Ada. "Carving a Niche: Visions of Gendered Childhood in Buchi Emecheta's *The Bride Price* & Tsitsi Dangarembga's *Nervous Conditions*." in Eldred Durosimi Jones and Marjorie Jones, ed. *Childhood in African Literature. African Literature Today* 21 Oxford: James Currey, 1998.

————. "Debunking Patriarchy: The Liberational Quality of Voicing in Tsitsi Dangarembga's *Nervous Conditions*." *Research in African Literatures* 26.1 (1995): 75-84.

Volet, Jean-Marie. "Calixthe Beyala, or the Literary Success of a Cameroonian Woman Living in Paris." *World Literature Today* 67 (1993): 309-14.

Walby, Sylvia. *Theorizing Patriarchy*. Oxford, England: Basil Blackwell, 1990.

Walker, Alice. *In Search of our Mothers' Gardens*. San Diego: Harcourt Brace Jovanovich, 1983.

Wilkinson, Jane. *Talking with African Writers: Interviews with African Poets, Playwrights and Novelists*. London: James Currey, 1992.

Willey, Ann Elizabeth, and Jeanette Treiber. *Negotiating the Postcolonial: Emerging Perspectives on Tsitsi Dangarembga*. Trenton, NJ: Africa World Press, 2002.

Yoder, Carroll. *White Shadows: A Dialectical View of the French African Novel*. Washington: Three Continents Press, 1990.